the lima collection

14 designs in Rowan Lima
by Marie Wallin & Sarah Hatton

Tallulah by Sarah Hatton

Backdrop - Red 'Marina' throw by Melin Tregwynt

Quinn by Marie Wallin
Sean Scarf by Sarah Hatton
Backdrop - Spice 'Marina' blanket by Melin Tregwynt

Brendalynn
by Sarah Hatton

Backdrop - Spice 'Marina' blanket by Melin Tregwynt

Alana by Sarah Hatton
Backdrop - Natural 'Marina' throw by Melin Tregwynt

Nathan
by Marie Wallin
Backdrop - Olive 'Waffle Tweed' throw by Melin Tregwynt

Rafferty by Sarah Hatton
Backdrop - Gold 'Marina' blanket by Melin Tregwynt

Maeve
by Marie Wallin

Backdrop - Olive 'Waffle Tweed' throw by Melin Tregwynt

Keira by Marie Wallin
Backdrop - Red 'Marina' throw by Melin Tregwynt

Aisling

by Marie Wallin

Backdrop - Gold 'Marina' blanket by Melin Tregwynt

Hildy by Marie Wallin
Backdrop - Spice 'Marina' blanket by Melin Tregwynt

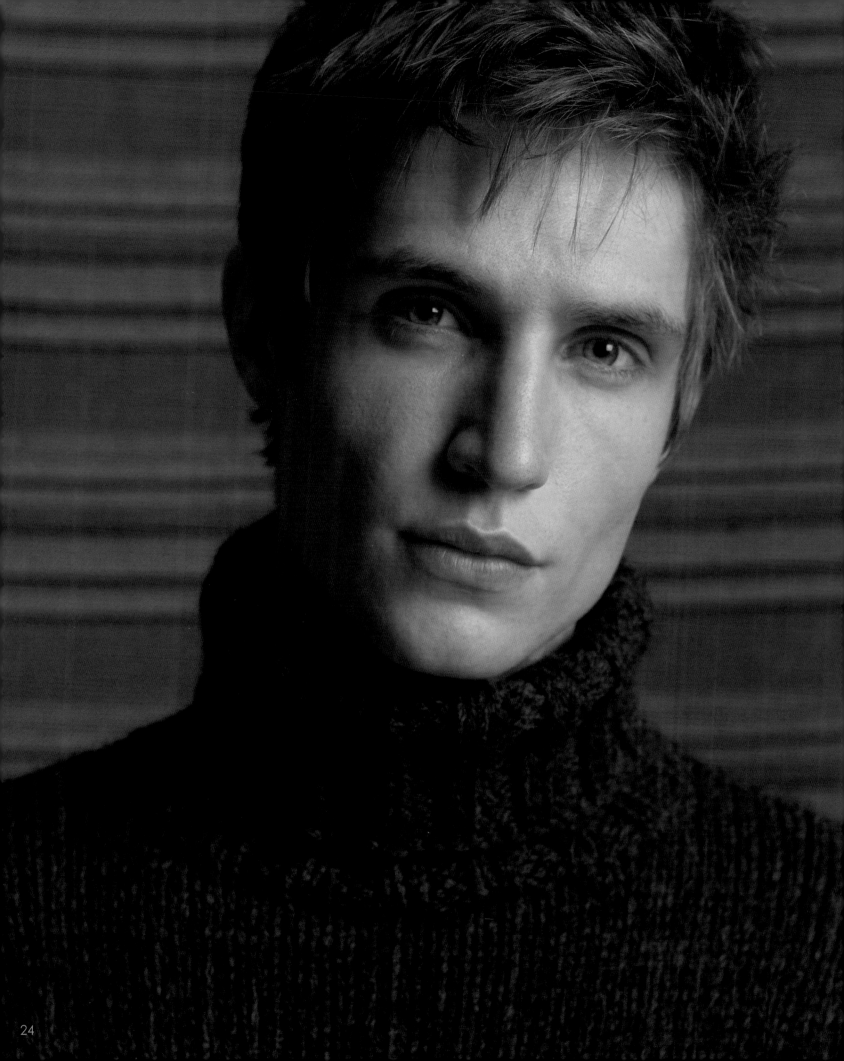

Backdrop - Natural 'Marina' throw by Melin Tregwynt

Deirdre by Marie Wallin
Backdrop - Spice 'Marina' blanket by Melin Tregwynt

Sean Wrap by Sarah Hatton
Backdrop - Olive 'Waffle Tweed' throw by Melin Tregwynt

Brea by Marie Wallin

Backdrop - Gold 'Marina' blanket by Melin Tregwynt

gallery

Brea   38

Dierdre *   48

Hildy   43

Quinn *   54

Sean Wrap   47

Rafferty   60

Alana *	36	Brody	46	Brendalynn *	40
Kiera	45	Maeve	50	Nathan	52
Tallulah *	57	Sean Scarf	47	Aisling	34

* The buttons for these designs are sourced from Bedecked. Please see credit page for contact details.

Aisling by Marie Wallin

SIZE	S	M	L	XL	XXL	
To fit bust						
	81–86	91–97	102–107	112–117	122–127	cm
	32–34	36–38	40–42	44–46	48–50	in

YARN

Rowan Lima

	12	13	14	15	17	x 50gm

(photographed in Chile 882)

NEEDLES

1 pair 5mm (no 6) (US 8) needles, 1 pair 5½mm (no 5) (US 9) needles, Stitch holder.

TENSION

20 sts and 26 rows to 10cm measured over st st using 5½ mm (no 5) (US 9) needles.

BACK

Using 5mm (US 8) needles cast on 91 [101: 113: 125: 139] sts.

Row 1 (RS): P2 [1: 1: 1: 2], ★ K3, P3, rep from ★ to last 5 [4: 4: 4: 5] sts, K3, P2 [1: 1: 1: 2].

Row 2: K2 [1: 1: 1: 2], P3, ★ K3, P3, rep from ★ to last 2 [1: 1: 1: 2] sts, K2 [1: 1: 1: 2].

These 2 rows form rib.

Work 36 rows more in rib dec 1 st at centre of last of these rows and ending with RS facing for next row. 90 [100: 112: 124: 138] sts.

Change to 5½mm (US 9) needles.

Beg with a K row, cont in st st shaping sides by dec 1 st at each end of 5th [9th: 11th: 13th: 15th] row, then on 3 foll 10th rows. 82 [92: 104: 116: 130] sts.

Work 15 rows straight, ending with RS facing for next row.

Inc 1 st at each end of next row, then on 3 foll 8th rows. 90 [100: 112: 124: 138] sts.

Cont straight until back meas 47 [48: 49: 50: 51] cm, ending with RS facing for next row.

Shape armholes

Cast off 4 [5: 7: 7: 9] sts at beg of next 2 rows. 82 [90: 98: 110: 120] sts.

Dec 1 st at each end of next 3 [5: 5: 7: 7] rows, then on foll 3 [3: 4: 5: 6] alt rows. 70 [74: 80: 86: 94] sts. ★★

Cont straight until armholes meas 22 [23: 24: 25: 26] cm, ending with RS facing for next row.

Shape shoulders and back neck

Cast off 5 [5: 6: 7: 8] sts at beg of next 2 rows. 60 [64: 68: 72: 78] sts.

Next row (RS): Cast off 5 [6: 6: 7: 8] sts, K until there are 8 [9: 10: 11: 12] sts on right hand needle, turn and leave rem sts on a stitch holder.

Work each side of neck separately.

Next row (WS): Cast off 3 sts, P to end.

Cast off rem 5 [6: 7: 8: 9] sts.

With RS facing, rejoin yarn to rem sts, cast off centre 34 [34: 36: 36: 38] sts, K to end.

Complete to match first side, reversing shapings.

FRONT

Work as given for back to ★★.

Cont straight until 26 [26: 28: 28: 30] rows less have been worked than on back to shoulder shaping, ending with RS facing for next row.

Divide for neck

Next row (RS): K27 [29: 31: 34: 37], turn and leave rem sts on stitch holder.

Work each side of neck separately.

Dec 1 st at neck edge of next 8 rows, then on 4 foll alt rows. 15 [17: 19: 22: 25] sts.

Work 9 [9: 11: 11: 13] rows, ending with RS facing for next row.

Shape shoulder

Cast off 5 [5: 6: 7: 8] sts at beg of next row, then 5 [6: 6: 7: 8] sts at beg of foll alt row.

Work 1 row.

Cast off rem 5 [6: 7: 8: 9] sts.

With RS facing rejoin yarn to rem sts left on a stitch holder, cast off centre 16 [16: 18: 18: 20] sts, K to end.

Complete to match first side, reversing shapings.

SLEEVES

Using 5mm (US 8) needles, cast on 41 [43: 45: 45: 47] sts.

Row 1 (RS): K0 [0: 0: 0: 1], P1 [2: 3: 3: 3], ★ K3, P3, rep from ★ to last 4 [5: 0: 0: 1] sts, K3 [3: 0: 0: 1], P1 [2: 0: 0: 0].

Row 2: P0 [0: 0: 0: 1], K1 [2: 3: 3: 3], ★ P3, K3, rep from ★ to last 4 [5: 0: 0: 1] sts, P3 [3: 0: 0: 0: 1], K1 [2: 0: 0: 0].

These 2 rows form rib.

Cont in rib shaping sides by inc 1 st at each end of 5th row, then on 4 foll 4th rows, working inc sts in rib. 51 [53: 55: 55: 57] sts.

Work 3 rows more, dec 1 st at centre of last of these rows. 50 [52: 54: 54: 56] sts.

Change to 5½mm (US 9) needles.

Beg with a K row, cont in st st shaping sides by inc 1 st at each end of next row, then on every foll 4th row to 62 [62: 62: 62: 64] sts, then every foll 6th row to 82 [84: 86: 86: 88] sts.

Cont straight until sleeve meas 46 [47: 48: 48: 48] cm, ending with RS facing for next row.

Shape top

Cast off 4 [5: 7: 7: 9] sts at beg of next 2 rows. 74 [74: 72: 72: 70] sts.
Dec 1 st at each end of next row, then on 3 [5: 8: 10: 13] foll alt rows, then every row to 40 sts.
Cast off 10 sts at beg of next 2 rows.
Cast off rem 20 sts.

MAKING UP

Press as described on the information page.
Join right shoulder seam.

Cowl neck

With RS facing and using 5mm (US 8) needles, pick up and knit 24 [24: 26: 26: 28] sts down left side of neck, 16 [16: 18: 18: 20] sts from front neck, 24 [24: 26: 26: 28] sts up right side of neck and 40 [40: 42: 42: 44] sts from back neck. 104 [104: 112: 112: 120] sts.

Next row (WS of garment, RS of cowl neck): P3 [3: 7: 7: 4], M1, (P7 [7: 7: 7: 8], M1) 14 times, P3 [3: 7: 7: 4]. 119 [119: 127: 127: 135] sts.

Next row: K1 [1: 0: 0: 0], P3 [3: 2: 2: 0], ★ K3, P3, rep from ★ to last 1 [1: 5: 5: 3] sts, K1 [1: 3: 3: 3], P0 [0: 2: 2: 0].

Next row: P1 [1: 0: 0: 0], K3 [3: 2: 2: 0], ★ P3, K3, rep from ★ to last 1 [1: 5: 5: 3] sts, P1 [1: 3: 3: 3], K0 [0: 2: 2: 0].

These 2 rows form rib.
Cont in rib until cowl neck meas 22 cm, ending with RS facing for next row.
Cast off in rib.

See information page for finishing instructions, setting in sleeves using the set-in method.

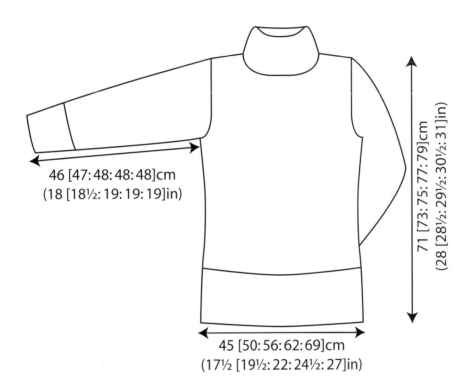

46 [47: 48: 48: 48]cm
(18 [18½: 19: 19: 19]in)

71 [73: 75: 77: 79]cm
(28 [28½: 29½: 30½: 31]in)

45 [50: 56: 62: 69]cm
(17½ [19½: 22: 24½: 27]in)

Alana by Sarah Hatton

SIZE	S	M	L	XL	XXL	
To fit bust						
	81–86	91–97	102–107	112–117	122–127	cm
	32–34	36–38	40–42	44–46	48–50	in
YARN						
Rowan Lima	9	9	10	11	12	x 50gm
(photographed in Nazca 887)						

NEEDLES
1 pair 5mm (no 6) (USA 8) needles, 1 pair 5½mm (no 5) (US 9) needles, Stitch holder.

EXTRAS
5 x BN1367 (18mm) buttons from Bedecked.

TENSION
20 sts and 26 rows to 10cm measured over st st using 5½mm (no 5) (US 9) needles.

BACK
Using 5½mm (US 9) needles cast on 90 [100: 112: 124: 138] sts.
Row 1 (RS): ★ K1, P1, rep from ★ to end.
Row 2: ★ P1, K1, rep from ★ to end.
These 2 rows form moss st.
Work 22 rows more in moss st, ending with RS facing for next row.
Beg with a K row, cont in st st as follows:
Dec 1 st at each end of 1st [1st: 5th: 9th: 11th] row, then on 2 foll 8th rows. 84 [94: 106: 118: 132] sts.
Work 13 rows straight, ending with RS facing for next row.
Inc 1 st at each end of next, then 2 foll 10th rows.
90 [100: 112: 124: 138] sts,
Work 9 rows, ending with RS facing for next row.
Work 4 rows in moss st.
Beg with a K row, cont in st st until back meas 35 [36: 37: 38: 39] cm, ending with RS facing for next row.
Shape raglan
Working in st st throughout cont as folls:
Cast off 2 [5: 7: 9: 11] sts at beg of next 2 rows.
86 [90: 98: 106: 116] sts.
Next row (RS): K1, sl 1, K1, psso, K to last 3 sts, K2tog, K1.
Next row: P1, P2tog, P to last 3 sts, P2togtbl, P1.
82 [86: 94: 102: 112] sts.
Dec 1 st at each end as before on next 1 [1: 5: 11: 15] rows, then on every foll alt row to 38 [38: 40: 40: 42] sts.
Work 1 row.
Cast off.

LEFT FRONT
Using 5½mm (US 9) needles cast on 42 [47: 53: 59: 66] sts.
Row 1 (RS): ★ K1, P1, rep from ★ to last 0 [1: 1: 1: 0] st, K0 [1: 1: 1: 0].
Row 2: K0 [1: 1: 1: 0], ★ P1, K1, rep from ★ to end.
These 2 rows form moss st.

Work 22 rows more in moss st, ending with RS facing for next row.
Beg with a K row, cont in st st as follows:
Dec 1 st at beg of 1st [1st: 5th: 9th: 11th] row, then 2 foll 8th rows. 39 [44: 50: 56: 63] sts.
Work 13 rows straight, ending with RS facing for next row.
Inc 1 st at each beg of next row, then 2 foll 10th rows.
42 [47: 53: 59: 66] sts.
Work 9 rows, ending with RS facing for next row.
Work 4 rows in moss st.
Beg with a K row, cont in st st until left front matches back to shape raglan, ending with RS facing for next row.
Shape raglan
Working in st st throughout cont as follows:
Next row (RS): Cast off 2 [5: 7: 9: 11] sts, patt to end.
40 [42: 46: 50: 55] sts.
Work 1 row.
Next row (RS): K1, sl 1, K1, psso, patt to end.
Next row: Patt to last 3 sts, P2togtbl, P1. 38 [40: 44: 48: 53] sts.
Dec 1 st at raglan edge as before on next 9 [9: 13: 19: 23] rows, then on 8 [10: 8: 6: 4] foll alt rows. 21 [21: 23: 23: 26] sts.
Shape neck
Next row (WS): Cast off 5 sts, patt to end. 16 [16: 18: 18: 21] sts.
Dec 1 st at raglan edge in next row, then on 4 [4: 4: 4: 3] foll alt rows **and at same time** dec 1 st at neck edge in every row.
2 [2: 4: 4: 10] sts.
Work 0 [0: 1: 1: 1] row straight.
Dec – [–: 1: 1: 1] st at each end of – [–: next: next: next] row, then – [–: –: –: 3] foll alt rows. 2 sts.
Next row (WS): P2tog.
Fasten off.

RIGHT FRONT
Using 5½mm (US 9) needles cast on 42 [47: 53: 59: 66] sts.
Row 1 (RS): K0 [1: 1: 1: 0], ★ P1, K1, rep from ★ to end.
Row 2: ★ K1, P1, rep from ★ to last 0 [1: 1: 1: 0] st, K0 [1: 1: 1: 0].

These 2 rows form moss st.

Work 22 rows more in moss st, ending with RS facing for next row.

Beg with a K row, cont in st st as folls:

Dec 1 st at end of 1st [1st: 5th: 9th: 11th] row, then on 2 foll 8th rows. 39 [44: 50: 56: 63] sts.

Complete to match left side reversing shapings.

SLEEVES

Using 5½mm (US 9) needles cast on 40 [42: 44: 46: 48] sts.

Work 18 rows in moss st as given for back, inc 1 st at each end of 5th row, then on 2 foll 6th rows, working inc sts in moss st. 46 [48: 50: 52: 54] sts.

Beg with a K row, cont in st st shaping sides by inc 1 st at each end of 5th [5th: 7th: 7th: 7th] row, then on every foll 6th [8th: 8th: 8th: 8th] row to 50 [72: 74: 76: 78] sts.

Size S only

Inc 1 st at each end of every foll 8th row to 70 sts.

All sizes

Cont straight until sleeve meas 46 [47: 48: 48: 48] cm, ending with RS facing for next row.

Shape raglan

Cast off 2 [5: 7: 9: 11] sts at beg of next 2 rows. 66 [62: 60: 58: 56] sts.

Working all decs as set by back cont as folls:

Dec 1 st at each end of next 13 [5: 1: 1: 1] rows, then – [–: –: 2: 5] foll 4th rows, then every foll alt row to 16 sts.

Work 1 row, ending with RS facing for next row.

Left sleeve only

Dec 1 st at beg of next row then cast off 7 sts at beg of foll row. 8 sts.

Dec 1 st at each end of next row, then 2 foll alt rows. 2 sts.

Next row (WS): P2tog. Fasten off.

Right sleeve only

Cast off 7 sts at beg and dec 1 st at end of next row. 8 sts.

Work 1 row.

Dec 1 st at each end of next row, then 2 foll alt rows. 2 sts.

Next row (WS): P2tog. Fasten off.

MAKING UP

Press as described on the information page.

Join raglan seams.

Neck edging

With RS facing and using 5mm (US 8) needles, pick up and knit 13 [13: 17: 17: 19] sts up right side of neck, 16 sts from right sleeve top, 38 [38: 40: 40: 42] sts from back neck, 16 sts from left sleeve top and 13 [13: 17: 17: 19] sts down left side of neck. 96 [96: 106: 106: 112] sts.

Work 12 rows in moss st as given for back, ending with **WS** facing for next row.

Cast off in moss st on **WS**.

Right front edging

With RS facing and using 5mm (US 8) needles, beg at start of st st and ending at neck edge, pick up and knit 62 [64: 64: 66: 66] sts evenly along front edge.

Work 3 rows in moss st as given for back, ending with RS facing for next row.

Next row (RS): Moss st 2 [3: 3: 2: 2] sts, cast off 2 sts (2 sts to be cast on over these 2 sts on foll row), (moss st 11 [11: 11: 12: 12] sts, cast off 2 sts) 4 times, moss st 1 [2: 2: 1: 1] sts.

Work 4 rows more, ending with **WS** facing for next row.

Cast off in moss st on **WS**.

Left front edging

With RS facing and using 5mm (US 8) needles beg at neck edge and ending at end of st st, pick up and knit 62 [64: 64: 66: 66] sts evenly along front edge.

Work as given for right front edging omitting buttonholes.

See information page for finishing instructions.

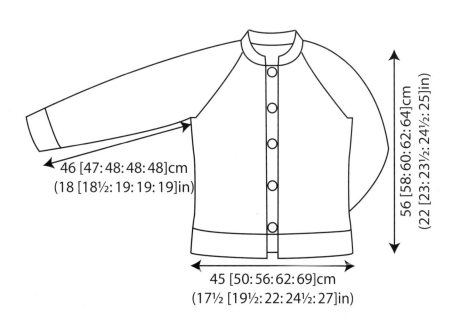

46 [47: 48: 48: 48]cm
(18 [18½: 19: 19: 19]in)

56 [58: 60: 62: 64]cm
(22 [23: 23½: 24½: 25]in)

45 [50: 56: 62: 69]cm
(17½ [19½: 22: 24½: 27]in)

SIZE	S	M	L	XL	XXL	
To fit bust						
	81–86	91–97	102–107	112–117	122–127	cm
	32–34	36–38	40–42	44–46	48–50	in

YARN

Rowan Lima

	12	13	14	15	17	x 50gm

(photographed in Lima 888)

NEEDLES

1 pair 5mm (no 6) (US 8) needles, 1 pair 5½mm (no 5) (US 9) needles, Stitch holder, Cable needle.

TENSION

26 sts and 26 rows to 10cm measured over patt and 20 sts and 26 rows over st st using 5½mm (no 5) (US 9) needles.

BACK

Using 5mm (US 8) needles cast on 108 [118: 130: 142: 156] sts.
Work 2 rows in g st.
Change to 5½mm (US 9) needles.
Beg with a K row, cont in st st until back meas 29 [30: 31: 32: 33] cm, ending with RS facing for next row.

Place yoke panel

Next row (RS): K17 [22: 28: 34: 41], work 74 sts from row 1 of chart, K17 [22: 28: 34: 41].
This row sets position of yoke panel.
Cont as set rep 4 rows of chart on centre 74 sts with st st at each side until back meas 37 [38: 39: 40: 41]cm, ending with RS facing for next row.

Shape armholes

Keeping patt correct cast off 4 [4: 4: 5: 6] sts at beg of next 2 rows.
100 [110: 122: 132: 144] sts.
Dec 1 st at each end of next 3 [5: 5: 5: 7] rows, then on foll 2 [2: 4: 5: 5] alt rows. 90 [96: 104: 112: 120] sts. ★★
Cont straight until armholes meas 22 [23: 24: 25: 26] cm, ending with RS facing for next row.

Shape shoulders and back neck

Keeping patt correct, cast off 7 [8: 9: 11: 11] sts at beg of next 2 rows.
76 [80: 86: 90: 98] sts.
Next row (RS): Cast off 8 [9: 10: 11: 12] sts, patt until there are 11 [12: 13: 14: 15] sts on right hand needle, turn and leave rem sts on a stitch holder.
Work each side of neck separately.
Next row (WS): Cast off 3 sts, patt to end.
Cast off rem 8 [9: 10: 11: 12] sts.
With RS facing rejoin yarn to rem sts, cast off centre 38 [38: 40: 40: 44] sts, patt to end.
Complete to match first side reversing shapings.

FRONT

Work as given for back to ★★.

Cont straight until 12 [12: 14: 14: 18] rows less have been worked than on back to shoulder shaping, ending with RS facing for next row.

Divide for neck

Next row (RS): Patt 31 [34: 37: 41: 44], turn and leave rem sts on stitch holder.
Work each side of neck separately.
Dec 1 st at neck edge of next 6 [6: 6: 6: 4] rows, then on 2 [2: 2: 2: 5] foll alt rows. 23 [26: 29: 33: 35] sts.
Work 1 [1: 3: 3: 3] rows, ending with RS facing for next row.

Shape shoulder

Keeping patt correct, cast off 7 [8: 9: 11: 11] sts at beg of next row, then 8 [9: 10: 11: 12] sts at beg of foll alt row.
Work 1 row.
Cast off rem 8 [9: 10: 11: 12] sts.
With RS facing, rejoin yarn to rem sts left on a stitch holder, cast off centre 28 [28: 30: 30: 32] sts, patt to end.
Complete to match first side, reversing shapings.

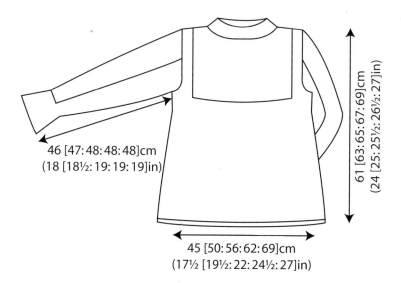

46 [47: 48: 48: 48]cm
(18 [18½: 19: 19: 19]in)

61 [63: 65: 67: 69]cm
(24 [25: 25½: 26½: 27]in)

45 [50: 56: 62: 69]cm
(17½ [19½: 22: 24½: 27]in)

SLEEVES

Using 5mm (US 8) needles, cast on 54 [54: 56: 56: 58] sts.

Work 2 rows in g st.

Change to 5½mm (US 9) needles

Beg with a K row, cont in st st until sleeve meas 7cm, ending with RS facing for next row.

Place sleeve panel

Next row (RS): K0 [0: 1: 1: 2], work 54 sts from row 1 of chart, K0 [0: 1: 1: 2].

This row sets position of sleeve panel.

Cont as set rep 4 rows of chart on centre 54 sts with st st at each side shaping sides by inc 1 st at each end of 2nd row, then on every foll 4th row to 90 [88: 88: 88: 90] sts, then every foll 6th row to 96 [96: 98: 98: 100] sts, working inc sts in st st.

Cont straight until sleeve meas 46 [47: 48: 48: 48] cm, ending with RS facing for next row.

Shape top

Keeping patt correct cast off 4 [4: 4: 5: 6] sts at beg of next 2 rows. 88 [88: 90: 88: 88] sts.

Dec 1 st at each end of next row, then on 4 [6: 7: 10: 12] foll alt rows, then every row to 56 sts.

Cast off 13 sts at beg of next 2 rows.

Cast off rem 30 sts.

MAKING UP

Press as described on the information page.

Join right shoulder seam.

Neckband

With RS facing and using 5mm (US 8) needles, pick up and knit 13 [13: 15: 15: 17] sts down left side of neck, 28 [28: 30: 30: 32] sts from front neck, 13 [13: 15: 15: 17] sts up right side of neck and 44 [44: 46: 46: 50] sts from back neck. 98 [98: 106: 106: 116] sts.

Cont in g st until neckband meas 3cm from pick up row, ending with **WS** facing for next row.

Cast off on **WS**.

See information page for finishing instructions, setting in sleeves using the set-in method.

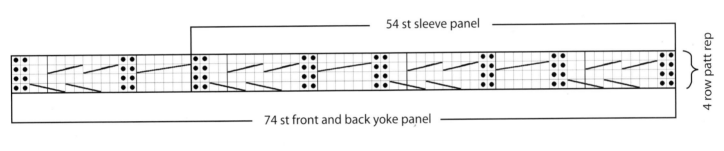

54 st sleeve panel

4 row patt rep

74 st front and back yoke panel

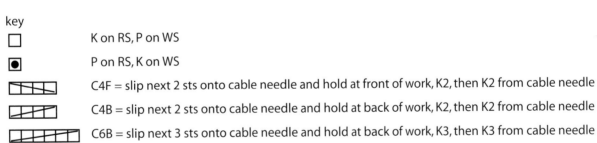

key

☐ K on RS, P on WS

▣ P on RS, K on WS

C4F = slip next 2 sts onto cable needle and hold at front of work, K2, then K2 from cable needle

C4B = slip next 2 sts onto cable needle and hold at back of work, K2, then K2 from cable needle

C6B = slip next 3 sts onto cable needle and hold at back of work, K3, then K3 from cable needle

SIZE To fit bust	S	M	L	XL	XXL	
	81–86	91–97	102–107	112–117	122–127	cm
	32–34	36–38	40–42	44–46	48–50	in
YARN						
Rowan Lima (photographed in Titicaca 883)	15	17	19	20	22	x 50gm

NEEDLES
1 pair 5mm (no 6) (US 8) needles, 1 pair 5½mm (no 5) (US 9) needles, Stitch holder.

EXTRAS
3 x BN1367 (25mm) buttons from Bedecked.

TENSION
20 sts and 26 rows to 10cm measured over patt using 5½mm (no 5) (US 9) needles.

BACK
Using 5mm (US 8) needles cast on 96 [106: 118: 130: 144] sts.
Work 4 rows in g st, ending with RS facing for next row.
Change to 5½mm (US 9) needles.
Beg and ending rows as indicated, repeating the 6 row patt from chart A, cont until back meas 25 [26: 27: 28: 29] cm, ending with RS facing for next row.
★ **Next row (RS)**: Purl.
Next row: Purl.
Beg and ending rows as indicated, work 19 rows from chart B, ending with **WS** facing for next row.
Work 3 rows in g st, ending with RS facing for next row. ★
Beg and ending rows as indicated, repeating the 6 row patt from chart C, cont until back meas 50 [51:52: 53: 54] cm, ending with RS facing for next row.
Work from ★ to ★ once more.
Beg and ending rows as indicated, repeating the 6 row patt from chart A throughout, cont until back meas 62 [63: 64: 65: 66] cm, ending with RS facing for next row.
Shape armholes
Keeping patt correct, cast off 4 [6: 9: 11: 14] sts at beg of next 2 rows. 88 [94: 100: 108: 116] sts.
Dec 1 st at each end of next 5 [7: 7: 9: 9] rows, then on foll 4 [3: 3: 2: 2] alt rows. 70 [74: 80: 86: 94] sts.
Cont straight in patt until armholes meas 21 [22: 23: 24: 25] cm, ending with RS facing for next row.
Shape shoulders and back neck
Cast off 4 [5: 5: 6: 7] sts at beg of next 2 rows. 62 [64: 70: 74: 80] sts.
Next row (RS): Cast off 4 [5: 6: 7: 8] sts, patt until there are 8 [8: 9: 10: 11] sts on right hand needle, turn and leave rem sts on a stitch holder.
Work each side of neck separately.
Next row (WS): Cast off 3 sts, patt to end.
Cast off rem 5 [5: 6: 7: 8] sts.
With RS facing rejoin yarn to rem sts, cast off centre 38 [38: 40:

40: 42] sts, patt to end.
Complete to match first side, reversing shapings.

POCKET LININGS (make 2)
Using 5½mm (US 9) needles cast on 26 sts.
Beg with a K row, work 35 rows in st st, ending with **WS** facing for next row.
Leave these 26 sts on a stitch holder.

LEFT FRONT
Using 5mm (US 8) needles cast on 52 [57: 63: 69: 76] sts.
Work 4 rows in g st, ending with RS facing for next row.
Change to 5½mm (US 9) needles.
Beg and ending rows as indicated, rep the 6 row patt from chart

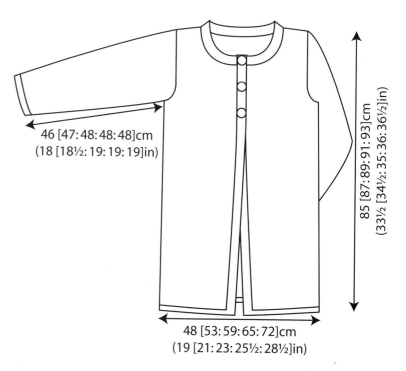

46 [47: 48: 48: 48]cm
(18 [18½: 19: 19: 19]in)

85 [87: 89: 91: 93]cm
(33½ [34½: 35: 36: 36½]in)

48 [53: 59: 65: 72]cm
(19 [21: 23: 25½: 28½]in)

A, work 45 [50: 56: 62: 69] sts from chart, turn and leave rem 7 sts on a stitch holder for front edging.

Cont in patt from chart A until left front meas 25 [26: 27: 28: 29] cm, ending with RS facing for next row.

★ **Next row (RS)**: Purl.

Next row: Purl.

Beg and ending rows as indicated, work 19 rows from chart B, ending with **WS** facing for next row. ★

Next row (WS): Knit.

Next row (place pocket): K5 [10: 16: 22: 29], cast off 26 sts, K to end.

Next row: K14, K across 26 sts on stitch holder with **WS** facing, K to end.

Beg and ending rows as indicated, rep the 6 row patt from chart C, cont until left front meas 50 [51:52: 53: 54] cm, ending with RS facing for next row.

Work from ★ to ★ once more.

Work 3 rows in g st, ending with RS facing for next row.

Beg and ending rows as indicated, rep the 6 row patt from chart A throughout, cont until left front matches back to shape armholes, ending with RS facing for next row.

Shape armhole

Next row (RS): Keeping patt correct, cast off 4 [6: 9: 11: 14] sts, patt to end. 41 [44: 47: 51: 55] sts.

Work 1 row.

Dec 1 st at armhole edge of next 5 [7: 7: 9: 9] rows, then on foll 4 [3: 3: 2: 2] alt rows. 32 [34: 37: 40: 44] sts.

Cont straight in patt until 29 [29: 33: 33: 35] rows less have been worked than on back to shape shoulders, ending with **WS** facing for next row.

Shape neck

Next row (WS): Keeping patt correct, cast off 7 sts, patt to end. 25 [27: 30: 33: 37] sts.

Dec 1 st at neck edge of next 7 rows, then 5 [5: 6: 6: 7] foll alt

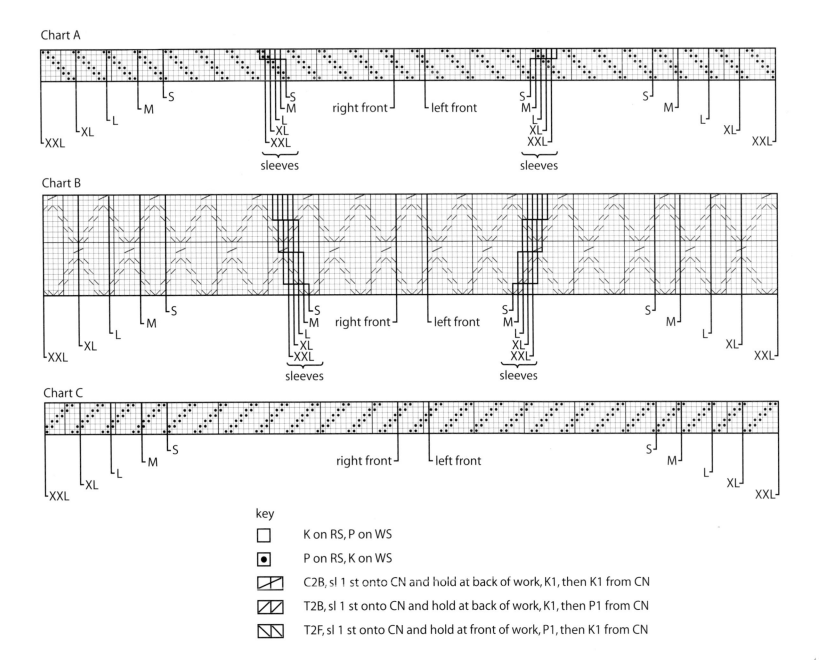

key

☐   K on RS, P on WS

⊡   P on RS, K on WS

▧   C2B, sl 1 st onto CN and hold at back of work, K1, then K1 from CN

▨   T2B, sl 1 st onto CN and hold at back of work, K1, then P1 from CN

◩   T2F, sl 1 st onto CN and hold at front of work, P1, then K1 from CN

rows. 13 [15: 17: 20: 23] sts.

Work 11 [11: 13: 13: 13] rows, ending with RS facing for next row.

Shape shoulder

Cast off 4 [5: 5: 6: 7] sts at beg of next row, then 4 [5: 6: 7: 8] sts at beg of foll alt row.

Cast off rem 5 [5: 6: 7: 8] sts.

RIGHT FRONT

Using 5mm (US 8) needles cast on 52 [57: 63: 69: 76] sts.

Work 4 rows in g st, ending with RS facing for next row.

Next row (RS): K7 and slip these sts onto a stitch holder for front edging.

Change to 5½mm (US 9) needles.

Beg and ending rows as indicated, rep the 6 row patt from chart A, cont on rem 45 [50: 56: 62: 69] sts until right front meas 25 [26: 27: 28: 29] cm, ending with RS facing for next row.

★ **Next row (RS)**: Purl.

Next row: Purl.

Beg and ending rows as indicated, work 19 rows from chart B, ending with **WS** facing for next row. ★

Next row (WS): Knit.

Next row (place pocket): K14, cast off 26 sts, K to end.

Next row: K5 [10: 16: 22: 29], K across 26 sts on stitch holder with **WS** facing, K to end.

Complete to match left side reversing shapings.

SLEEVES

Using 5mm (US 8) needles cast on 40 [42: 44: 46: 48] sts.

Work 4 rows in g st, ending with RS facing for next row.

Change to 5½mm (US 9) needles.

Beg and ending rows as indicated, work 19 rows in patt from chart B **and at same time** inc 1 st at each end of 3rd row, then 2 foll 6th rows. 46 [48: 50: 52: 54] sts.

Work 3 rows in g st, inc 1 st at each end of 2nd of these rows, ending with RS facing for next row. 48 [50: 52: 54: 56] sts.

Cont in patt from chart A throughout **and at same time** shaping sides by inc 1 st at each end of 5th row, then on every foll 6th [6th: –: –: –] row to 54 [54: –: –: –] sts, then on every foll 8th row to 70 [72: 74: 76: 78] sts, working inc sts in patt.

Cont straight until sleeve meas 46 [47: 48: 48: 48] cm, ending with RS facing for next row.

Shape top

Keeping patt correct cast off 4 [6: 9: 11: 14] sts at beg of next 2 rows. 62 [60: 56: 54: 50] sts.

Dec 1 st at each end of next 5 [3: 1: 1: 1] rows, then on foll 10 [13: 15: 16: 17] alt rows, then on every row to 26 [26: 22: 18: 12] sts.

Cast off 6 [6: 5: 4: 2] sts at beg of next 2 rows.

Cast off rem 14 [14: 12: 10: 8] sts.

MAKING UP

Press as described on the information page.

Join shoulder seams.

Neck edging

With RS facing and using 5mm (US 8) needles pick up and knit 35 [35: 37: 37: 39] sts up right side of neck, 44 [44: 46: 46: 48] sts from back neck and 35 [35: 37: 37: 39] sts down left side of neck.

114 [114: 120: 120: 126] sts.

Work 10 rows in g st, ending with **WS** facing for next row.

Cast off on **WS**.

Left front edging

With RS facing and using 5mm (US 8) needles rejoin yarn to 7 sts left on a stitch holder and cont in garter st until left front edging matches left front to cast off edge of neck edging when slightly stretched, ending with **WS** facing for next row. Cast off on **WS**.

Slip stitch to left front and place markers for buttons, the first to be 2 cm from cast off edge of neckband, the third to be 20 cm below and the second halfway between.

Right front edging

With **WS** facing and using 5mm (US 8) needles rejoin yarn to 7 sts left on a stitch holder and complete as given for left front edging working buttonholes to correspond with markers as foll:

Buttonhole row (RS): K3, cast off 2 sts (2 sts to be cast on over these 2 sts on foll row), K1.

Slip stitch pocket linings flat to inside of garment.

See information page for finishing instructions, setting in sleeves using the set-in method.

Hildy by Marie Wallin

SIZE	S	M	L	XL	XXL	
To fit bust						
	81-86	91-96	102-107	112-117	122-127	cm
	32-34	36-38	40-42	44-46	48-50	in

YARN
Rowan Lima

| | 17 | 18 | 20 | 21 | 22 | x 50gm |

(photographed in Machu Picchu 885)

NEEDLES
1 pair 5mm (no 6) (US 8), 1 pair 5½mm (no 5) (US 9) needles, Stitch holders.

TENSION
24 sts and 26 rows to 10cm measured over patt using 5½mm (no 5) (US 9) needles.

BACK

Using 5mm (US 8) needles cast on 129 [141: 159: 171: 189] sts.
Row 1 (RS): ★ K3, P3, rep from ★ to last 3 sts, K3.
Row 2: P3, ★ K3, P3, rep from ★ to end.
These 2 rows form rib.
Work 16 rows more in rib, dec – [–: 4: –: 2] sts evenly across last of these rows. 129 [141: 155: 171: 187] sts.
Change to 5½mm (US 9) needles.
Row 1 (RS): K1 [7: 6: 6: 6], ★ P5, K1, P1, K1, rep from ★ to last 0 [6: 5: 5: 5] sts, K0 [6: 5: 5: 5].
Row 2: P1 [7: 6: 6: 6], ★ M1, (K1, P1, K1) into next st, M1, P1, P5tog, P1, rep from ★ to last 0 [6: 5: 5: 5] sts, P0 [6: 5: 5: 5].
Row 3: K1 [7: 6: 6: 6], ★ P1, K1, P5, K1, rep from ★ to last 0 [6: 5: 5: 5] sts, K0 [6: 5: 5: 5].
Row 4: P1 [7: 6: 6: 6], ★ K5, P1, K1, P1, rep from ★ to last 0 [6: 5: 5: 5] sts, P0 [6: 5: 5: 5].
Row 5: As row 3.
Row 6: As row 4.
Row 7: As row 3.
Row 8: P1 [7: 6: 6: 6], ★ P5tog, P1, M1, (K1, P1, K1) into next st, M1, P1, rep from ★ to last 0 [6: 5: 5: 5] sts, P0 [6: 5: 5: 5].
Row 9: As row 1.
Row 10: P1 [7: 6: 6: 6], ★ K1, P1, K5, P1, rep from ★ to last 0 [6: 5: 5: 5] sts, P0 [6: 5: 5: 5].
Row 11: As row 1.
Row 12: As row 10.
These 12 rows form patt.
Cont in patt as set until back meas 42 [42: 42: 43: 44] cm, ending with RS facing for next row.
Shape sleeves
Cont in patt, inc 1 st at each end of next 5 [7: 9: 9: 9] rows, working inc sts in patt.
139 [155: 173: 189: 205] sts.
Cont straight in patt until armholes meas 25 [26: 27: 28: 29] cm from last inc row ending with RS facing for next row.

Shape shoulders
Cast off 14 [16: 19: 22: 24] sts at beg of next 2 rows, then 15 [18: 20: 23: 25] sts at beg of next 2 rows and 15 [18: 21: 23: 26] sts at beg of next 2 rows.
Leave rem 51 [51: 53: 53: 55] sts on a stitch holder.

LEFT FRONT

Using 5mm (US 8) needles cast on 105 [111: 117: 123: 135] sts.
Work 17 rows in rib as given for back, ending with **WS** facing for next row.
Next row (WS): Rib 36 sts and leave these sts on a stitch holder for front edging, rib2tog, (rib18 [18: 18: 0: 18], rib2tog) 3 [3: 2: 0: 4] times, rib to end.
Cont on these 65 [71: 78: 86: 94] sts only.
Change to 5½mm (US 9) needles.
Row 1 (RS): K1 [7: 6: 6: 6], ★ P5, K1, P1, K1, rep from ★ to end.
Row 2: P1, ★ M1, (K1, P1, K1) into next st, M1, P1, P5tog, P1, rep from ★ to last 0 [6: 5: 5: 5] sts, P0 [6: 5: 5: 5].
Row 3: K1 [7: 6: 6: 6], ★ P1, K1, P5, K1, rep from ★ to end.
Row 4: P1, ★ K5, P1, K1, P1, rep from ★ to last 0 [6: 5: 5: 5] sts, P0 [6: 5: 5: 5].
Row 5: As row 3.
Row 6: As row 4.
Row 7: As row 3.
Row 8: P1, ★ P5tog, P1, M1, (K1, P1, K1) into next st, M1, P1, rep from ★ to last 0 [6: 5: 5: 5] sts, P0 [6: 5: 5: 5].
Row 9: As row 1.
Row 10: P1, ★ K1, P1, K5, P1, rep from ★ to last 0 [6: 5: 5: 5] sts, P0 [6: 5: 5: 5].
Row 11: As row 1.
Row 12: As row 10.
These 12 rows form patt.
Cont in patt as set until left front matches back to shape sleeves, ending with RS facing for next row.

43

Shape sleeve

Inc 1 st at beg of next row and at same edge on foll 4 [6: 8: 8: 8] rows, working inc sts in patt. 70 [78: 87: 95: 103] sts.

Cont straight in patt until left front matches back to shape shoulders, ending with RS facing for next row.

Shape shoulder

Cast off 14 [16: 19: 22: 24] sts at beg of next row, then 15 [18: 20: 23: 25] at beg of foll alt row and 15 [18: 21: 23: 26] sts at beg of foll alt row.

Work 1 row.

Cast off rem 26 [26: 27: 27: 28] sts.

RIGHT FRONT

Using 5mm (US 8) needles cast on 105 [111: 117: 123: 135] sts.

Work 17 rows in rib as given for back, ending with **WS** facing for next row.

Next row (WS): Rib 7 [13: 39: 85: 17], rib2tog, (rib 18 [18: 18: 0: 18], rib2tog) 3 [3: 2: 0: 4] times, slip rem 36 sts onto a stitch holder for front edging turn and work on these 65 [71: 78: 86: 94] sts only.

Change to 5½mm (US 9) needles

Row 1 (RS): K1, ★ P5, K1, P1, K1, rep from ★ to last 0 [6: 5: 5: 5] sts, K0 [6: 5: 5: 5].

Row 2: P1 [7: 6: 6: 6], ★ M1, (K1, P1, K1) into next st, M1, P1, P5tog, P1, rep from ★ to end.

Row 3: K1, ★ P1, K1, P5, K1, rep from ★ to last 0 [6: 5: 5: 5] sts, K0 [6: 5: 5: 5].

Row 4: P1 [7: 6: 6: 6], ★ K5, P1, K1, P1, rep from ★ to end.

Row 5: As row 3.

Row 6: As row 4.

Row 7: As row 3.

Row 8: P1 [7: 6: 6: 6], ★ P5tog, P1, M1, (K1, P1, K1) into next st, M1, P1, rep from ★ to end.

Row 9: As row 1.

Row 10: P1 [7: 6: 6: 6], ★ K1, P1, K5, P1, rep from ★ to end.

Row 11: As row 1.

Row 12: As row 10.

These 12 rows form patt.

Complete to match left side, reversing shapings.

MAKING UP

Press as described on the information page.

Join shoulder seams. Join side and sleeve seams.

Left front edging

With RS facing and using 5mm (US 8) needles, rejoin yarn to 36 sts left on stitch holder and cont in rib until front edging fits to back

stitch holder, slip stitching to front and ending with RS facing for next row. Place these 36 sts onto a second stitch holder.

Right front edging

With **WS** facing and using 5mm (US 8) needles, rejoin yarn to 36 sts left on a stitch holder. Work as given for left front edging.

Collar

With RS facing, place 36 sts from left front edge, 51 [51: 53: 53: 55] sts from back neck and 36 sts from right front edge onto left needle. 123 [123: 125: 125: 127] sts.

Row 1 (RS): ★ K3, P3, rep from ★ to last 3 sts, K3.

Row 2: P3, ★ K3, rep from ★ to end.

These 2 rows form rib.

Work 16 rows more in rib, ending with RS facing for next row. Cast off in rib.

Cuff trim (make 2)

Using 5mm (US 8) needles cast on 117 [123: 129: 135: 141] sts.

Cont in rib as given for back until cuff trim meas 16cm, ending with RS facing for next row.

Cast off in rib.

Tie

Using 5mm (US 8) needles cast on 15 sts.

Cont in rib as given for back until tie meas 150 [160: 170: 180: 190] cm, ending with RS facing for next row.

Cast off in rib.

Join row end edges of cuff trim and slip stitch to row end edges of sleeves matching cuff trim seam to side seam of garment. Fold in half onto right side.

See information page for finishing instructions.

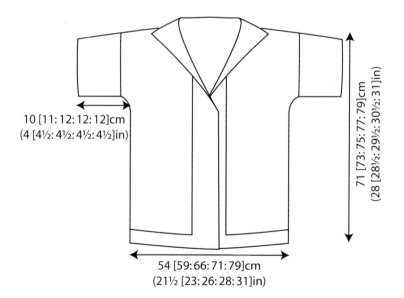

10 [11: 12: 12: 12]cm
(4 [4½: 4½: 4½: 4½]in)

71 [73:75: 77:79]cm
(28 [28½: 29½: 30½: 31]in)

54 [59:66: 71:79]cm
(21½ [23: 26: 28: 31]in)

Keira by Marie Wallin

SIZE To fit bust	S	M	L	XL	
	81–86	91–96	102–107	112–117	cm
	32–34	36–38	40–42	44–46	in

YARN

Rowan Lima

	11	12	13	15	x 50gm

(photographed in Cusco 884)

NEEDLES

1 pair 5½mm (no 5) (US 9) needles.

TENSION

23 sts and 24 rows to 10cm measured over patt using 5½mm (no 5) (US 9) needles.

MAIN SECTION

Using 5½mm (US 9) needles cast on 70 [80: 92: 104] sts.
Beg and ending rows as indicated, rep the 12 row patt from chart A, noting that row 1 is a **WS** row, cont until main section meas 156 [166: 176: 186] cm, ending with RS facing for next row.
Cast off.

BACK

Using 5½mm (US 9) needles cast on 30 [40: 50: 60] sts.
Beg and ending rows as indicated, rep the 12 row patt from chart B, noting that row 1 is a **WS** row, cont until back meas 33 cm, ending with RS facing for next row.
Cast off.

SLEEVES

Using 5½mm (US 9) needles cast on 56 [58: 60: 62] sts.
Beg and ending rows as indicated, rep the 12 row patt from chart A, noting that row 1 is a **WS** row, inc 1 st at each end of 4th row, then on every foll 4th row to 82 [80: 80: 82] sts, then on every foll 6th row to 98 [100: 102: 104] sts working inc sts in patt.
Cont straight until sleeve meas 47 [48: 49: 49] cm, ending with RS facing for next row.
Cast off.

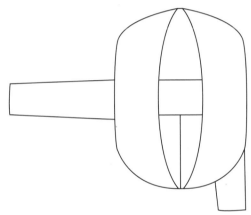

MAKING UP

Press as described on the information page. Join sleeve seams.
Join cast on and cast off edges of main section using back stitch or mattress st if preferred. Placing seam at centre, join main section to one of row end edges of back (this forms lower back seam).
Fold main section in half to find centre point. Matching this point to centre of back, join to opposite row end edge.
Placing sleeve seams 8 [9: 10: 11] cm from lower back seams, join sleeves to cast on and cast off edges of back and remaining main section edges.
See information page for finishing instructions.

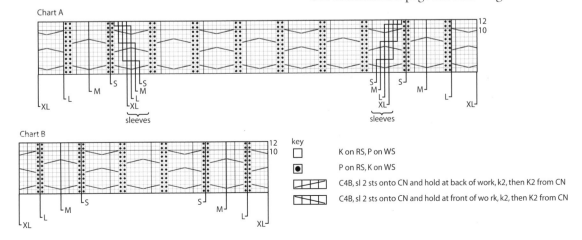

Chart A

Chart B

key

☐ K on RS, P on WS

⊙ P on RS, K on WS

C4B, sl 2 sts onto CN and hold at back of work, k2, then K2 from CN

C4B, sl 2 sts onto CN and hold at front of wo rk, k2, then K2 from CN

■ Brody by Marie Wallin

SIZE	S	M	L	XL	XXL	2XL	
To fit chest							
	102	107	112	117	122	127	cm
	40	42	44	46	48	50	in

YARN

Rowan Lima

	18	19	21	22	24	25	x 50gm

(photographed in Patagonia 878)

NEEDLES

1 pair 7mm (no 2) (US 10½) needles, 1 pair 8mm (no 0) (US 11) needles, Stitch holder.

TENSION

12.5 sts and 16.5 rows to 10cm measured over st st using 8 mm (no 0) (US 11) needles and **2 ends of yarn.**

BACK

Using 7mm (US 10½) needles and **2 ends of yarn** cast on 70 [74: 78: 82: 86: 90] sts.

Row 1 (RS): ★ K2, P2, rep from ★ to last 2 sts, K2.

Row 2: P2, ★ K2, P2, rep from ★ to end.

These 2 rows form rib.

Work 10 rows more in rib, dec 0 [0: 0: 0: 0: 2] sts evenly across last of these rows, ending with RS facing for next row.

70 [74: 78: 82: 86: 88] sts.

Change to 8mm (US 11) needles.

Beg with a K row, cont in st st until back meas 37 [38: 37: 38: 37: 38] cm, ending with RS facing for next row.

Shape armholes

Dec 1 st at each end of next 4 [4: 3: 3: 2: 1] rows.

62 [66: 72: 76: 82: 86] sts. ★★

Cont straight until armholes meas 26 [27: 28: 29: 30: 31] cm, ending with RS facing for next row.

Shape shoulders and back neck

Cast off 6 [7: 7: 8: 9: 9] sts at beg of next 2 rows.

50 [52: 58: 60: 64: 68] sts.

Next row (RS): Cast off 6 [7: 8: 8: 9: 10] sts, K until there are 10 [10: 11: 12: 12: 13] sts on right hand needle, turn and leave rem sts on a stitch holder.

Work each side of neck separately.

Next row (WS): Cast off 3 sts, P to end.

Cast off rem 7 [7: 8: 9: 9: 10] sts.

With RS facing, rejoin yarn to rem sts, cast off centre 18 [18: 20: 20: 22: 22] sts, K to end.

Complete to match first side reversing shapings.

FRONT

Work as given for back to ★★.

Cont straight until 4 [4: 6: 6: 8: 8] rows less have been worked than on back to shoulder shaping, ending with RS facing for next row.

Divide for neck

Next row (RS): K22 [24: 27: 29: 32: 34], turn and leave rem sts on stitch holder.

Work each side of neck separately.

Dec 1 st at neck edge of next 3 [3: 4: 4: 5: 5] rows.

19 [21: 23: 25: 27: 29] sts.

Work 0 [0: 1: 1: 2: 2] rows, ending with RS facing for next row.

Shape shoulder

Cast off 6 [7: 7: 8: 9: 9] sts at beg of next row, then 6 [7: 8: 8: 9: 10] sts at beg of foll alt row.

Work 1 row.

Cast off rem 7 [7: 8: 9: 9: 10] sts.

With RS facing, rejoin yarn to rem sts left on a stitch holder, cast off centre 18 sts, K to end.

Complete to match first side reversing shapings.

SLEEVES

Using 7mm (US 10½) needles and **2 ends of yarn**, cast on 30 [30: 34: 34: 38: 38] sts.

Work 12 rows in rib as given for back, shaping sides by inc 1 st at each end of 5th row, then on foll 4th row and dec 2 [0: 2: 0: 2: 0] sts evenly across last of these rows. 32 [34: 36: 38: 40: 42] sts.

Change to 8mm (US 11) needles.

Beg with a K row, cont in st st shaping sides by inc 1 st at each end of next row then on every foll 4th row to 52 [52: 50: 48: 48: 46] sts, then every foll 6th row to 62 [64: 66: 68: 70: 72] sts.

Cont straight until sleeve meas 53 [55: 57: 59: 61: 63] cm, ending with RS facing for next row.

Shape top

Dec 1 st at each end of next 12 [14: 16: 18: 20: 22] rows.

Cast off rem 38 [36: 34: 32: 30: 28] sts.

MAKING UP

Press as described on the information page.

Join right shoulder seam.

Polo neck

With RS facing and using 7mm (US 10½) needles and **2 ends of yarn**, pick up and knit 8 [8: 9: 9: 10: 10] sts down left side of neck, 18 sts from front neck, 8 [8: 9: 9: 10: 10] sts up right side of neck and 24 [24: 26: 26: 28: 28] sts from back neck.
58 [58: 62: 62: 66: 66] sts.
Beg with row 2 of rib as given for back, cont in rib until polo neck meas 11 cm.
Change to 8mm (US 11) needles.
Cont until polo neck meas 22 cm, ending with RS facing for next row.
Cast off in rib.
Join left shoulder and polo neck seams, reversing stitching for last 11cm of polo neck.
See information page for finishing instructions, setting in sleeves using the shallow set-in method.

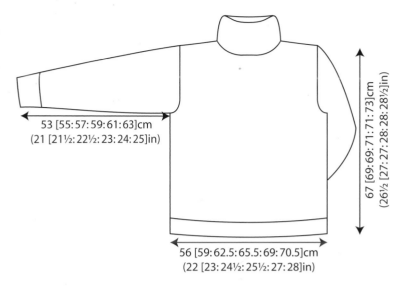

53 [55: 57: 59: 61: 63]cm
(21 [21½: 22½: 23: 24: 25]in)

67 [69: 69: 71: 71: 73]cm
(26½ [27: 27: 28: 28: 28½]in)

56 [59: 62.5: 65.5: 69: 70.5]cm
(22 [23: 24½: 25½: 27: 28]in)

■■□ Sean by Sarah Hatton

YARN
Rowan Lima
Mens scarf   4 x 50gm
(photographed in Pampas 881 & Lima 888)
Womens wrap   9 x 50gm
(photographed in Chile 882 & Machu Picchu 885)

SIZE
Mens scarf   21 x 158 cm (8½ x 62 in), Womens wrap 54 x 190 cm (21½ x 75 in)

NEEDLES
1 pair 5½mm (no 5) (US 9) needles

TENSION
20 sts and 26 rows to 10cm measured over st st, 18 sts and 26 rows measured over patt on 5½mm (US 9) needles.

MENS SCARF
Using 5½mm (US 9) needles, cast on 37 sts.
Row 1 (RS): K1, ★ P3, K1, rep from ★ to end.
Row 2: K4, ★ P1, K3, rep from ★ to last st, K1.
Row 3: As row 1.
Row 4: K1, ★ yfwd, K3tog, yrn, P1, rep from ★ to last 4 sts, yfwd, K3tog, yfwd, K1.
Row 5: K1, ★ P1, K1, P2, rep from ★ to last 4 sts, (P1, K1) twice.
Row 6: K2, P1, K1, ★ K2, P1, K1, rep from ★ to last st, K1.
Row 7: As row 5.
Row 8: K2, P1, ★ yfwd, K3tog, yrn, P1, rep from ★ to last 2 sts, K2.
These 8 rows set patt.
Cont in patt as set until scarf meas 158 cm, ending with row 2 or 6.
Cast off in patt.

WOMENS WRAP
Using 5½mm (US 9) needles, cast on 97 sts.
Work in patt as set on Mens scarf until work meas 190 cm, ending with row 2 or 6.
Cast off in patt.

Deirdre by Marie Wallin

SIZE To fit bust	S	M	L	XL	XXL	
	81–86	91–97	102–107	112–117	122–127	cm
	32–34	36–38	40–42	44–46	48–50	in
YARN						
Rowan Lima (photographed in Peru 889)	17	19	21	23	25	x 50gm

NEEDLES

5½mm (no 5) (US 9) circular needle, 1 pair 5½mm (no 5) (US 9) needles, Cable needle, Stitch holder.

EXTRAS

4 x BN1366 (15mm) buttons from Bedecked.

TENSION

22 sts and 26 rows to 10cm measured over moss st patt and 23 sts and 27 rows over cable patt using 5½mm (no 5) (US 9) needles.

BACK

Using 5½mm (US 9) circular needle cast on 167 [195: 209: 239: 255] sts.

Row 1 (RS): ★ K1, P1, rep from ★ to last st, K1.

This row forms moss st.

Work 3 rows more in moss st.

Row 1 (RS): (K1, P1) 6 [3: 6: 3: 7] times, K1 [0: 1: 1: 1], (work 21 sts from row 1 of cable and moss st patt panel on chart) 7 [9: 9: 11: 11] times, K1 [0: 1: 1: 1], (P1, K1) 3 [0: 3: 0: 4] times.

Row 2: (K1, P1) 3 [0: 3: 0: 4] times, K1 [0: 1: 1: 1], (work 21 sts from row 2 of cable and moss st patt panel on chart) 7 [9: 9: 11: 11] times, K1 [0: 1: 1: 1], (P1, K1) 6 [3: 6: 3: 7] times.

These 2 rows set patt – 21 sts of cable and moss st panel patt which is repeated with moss st either side.

Cont in patt as set, rep 20 rows from chart until back meas 37 [38: 39: 40: 41] cm, ending with RS facing for next row.

Next row (RS): (K1, P1) 6 [3: 6: 3: 7] times, K1 [0: 1: 1: 1], (K2tog, (K3tog) 4 times, K1, (K1, P1) 3 times) 7 [9: 9: 11: 11] times, K1 [0: 1: 1: 1], (P1, K1) 3 [0: 3: 0: 4] times. 104 [114: 128: 140: 156] sts.

Yoke pattern

Next row (WS): (K1, P1) 6 [3: 6: 3: 7] times, K1 [0: 1: 1: 1], (P6, (P1, K1) 3 times) 6 [8: 8: 10: 10] times, P6, K1 [0: 1: 1: 1], (P1, K1) 6 [3: 6: 3: 7] times.

Next row (RS): (K1, P1) 6 [3: 6: 3: 7] times, K1 [0: 1: 1: 1], (K6, (K1, P1) 3 times) 7 [9: 9: 11: 11] times, K1 [0: 1: 1: 1], (P1, K1) 3 [0: 3: 0: 4] times.

These 2 rows set yoke patt.

Cont in yoke patt as set until back meas 47 [48: 49: 50: 51] cm, ending with RS facing for next row.

Shape armholes

Keeping patt correct cast off 5 [7: 8: 9: 11] sts at beg of next 2 rows. 94 [100: 112: 122: 134] sts.

Dec 1 st at each end of next 3 [3: 5: 5: 7] rows, then foll 3 [4: 5: 6: 7] alt rows. 82 [86: 92: 100: 106] sts.

Cont straight in patt until armholes meas 22 [23: 24: 25: 26] cm,

ending with RS facing for next row.

Shape shoulders and back neck

Cast off 5 [6: 7: 8: 9] sts at beg of next 2 rows, 6 [6: 7: 8: 9] sts at beg of next 2 rows and 6 [7: 7: 9: 9] sts at beg of next 2 rows. 48 [48: 50: 50: 52] sts.

Cont on these sts for a further 20 cm, to form collar, ending with RS facing for next row.

Cast off.

LEFT FRONT

Using 5½mm (US 9) needles cast on 97 [111: 118: 133: 141] sts.

Row 1 (RS): ★ K1, P1, rep from ★ to last 1 [1: 2: 1: 1] sts, K1, P0 [0: 1: 0: 0].

Row 2: P0 [0: 1: 0: 0], ★ K1, P1, rep from ★ to last st, K1.

These 2 rows form moss st.

Work 2 rows more in moss st.

Row 1 (RS): (K1, P1) 6 [3: 6: 3: 7] times, K1 [0: 1: 1: 1], (work 21 sts from row 1 of cable and moss st patt panel on chart) 4 [5: 5: 6: 6] times.

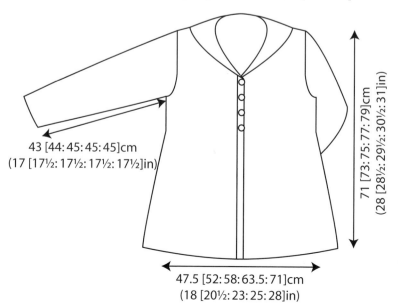

43 [44: 45: 45: 45]cm
(17 [17½: 17½: 17½: 17½]in)

71 [73: 75: 77: 79]cm
(28 [28½: 29½: 30½: 31]in)

47.5 [52: 58: 63.5: 71]cm
(18 [20½: 23: 25: 28]in)

Row 2: (Work 21 sts from row 2 of cable and moss st patt panel on chart) 4 [5: 5: 6: 6] times, K1 [0: 1: 1: 1], (P1, K1) 6 [3: 6: 3: 7] times.

These 2 rows set patt – 21 sts of cable and moss st panel patt which is repeated with moss st at side edge.

Cont in patt as set rep 20 rows from chart until left front meas 37 [38: 39: 40: 41] cm, ending with RS facing for next row.

Next row (RS): (K1, P1) 6 [3: 6: 3: 7] times, K1 [0: 1: 1: 1], (K2tog, (K3tog) 4 times, K1, (K1, P1) 3 times) 4 [5: 5: 6: 6] times. 61 [66: 73: 79: 87] sts.

Yoke pattern

Next row (WS): (P1, K1) 3 times, (P6, (P1, K1) 3 times) 3 [4: 4: 5: 5] times, P6, K1 [0: 1: 1: 1], (P1, K1) 6 [3: 6: 3: 7] times.

Next row (RS): (K1, P1) 6 [3: 6: 3: 7] times, K1 [0: 1: 1: 1], (K6, (K1, P1) 3 times) 4 [5: 5: 6: 6] times.

These 2 rows set yoke patt.

Cont in yoke patt as set until left front matches back to shape armholes, ending with RS facing for next row.

Shape armhole

Next row (RS): Keeping patt correct cast off 5 [7: 8: 9: 11] sts, patt to end. 56 [59: 65: 70: 76] sts.

Work 1 row.

Dec 1 st at armhole edge of next 3 [3: 5: 5: 7] rows, then on foll 3 [4: 5: 6: 7] alt rows. 50 [52: 55: 59: 62] sts.

Cont straight until left front matches back to shape shoulders, ending with RS facing for next row.

Shape shoulder

Cast off 5 [6: 7: 8: 9] sts at beg of next row, then 6 [6: 7: 8: 9] sts at beg of foll alt row, then 6 [7: 7: 9: 9] sts at beg of foll alt row. 33 [33: 34: 34: 35] sts.

Cont on these sts for a further 20 cm to form collar, ending with RS facing for next row.

Cast off.

Mark position of 4 buttons on left front opening edge, first to come in row 4 of yoke patt, last to come 30 cm below collar cast off edge and rem 2 buttons spaced evenly between.

RIGHT FRONT

Using 5½mm (US 9) needles cast on 97 [111: 118: 133: 141] sts.

Row 1 (RS): P0 [0: 1: 0: 0], ★ K1, P1, rep from ★ to last st, K1.

Row 2: ★ K1, P1, rep from ★ to last 1 [1: 2: 1: 1] sts, K1, P0 [0: 1: 0: 0].

This 2 rows form moss st.

Work 2 rows more in moss st.

Row 1 (RS): (K1, P1) 3 times, (work 21 sts from row 1 of cable and moss st patt panel on chart) 4 [5: 5: 6: 6] times, K1 [0: 1: 1: 1], (P1, K1) 3 [0: 3: 0: 4] times.

Row 2: (K1, P1) 3 [0: 3: 0: 4] times, K1 [0: 1: 1: 1], (work 21 sts from row 2 of cable and moss st patt panel on chart) 4 [5: 5: 6: 6] times, (P1, K1) 3 times.

These 2 rows set patt – 21 sts of cable and moss st panel patt which is repeated with moss st at side edge.

Cont in patt as set, rep 20 rows from chart until right front meas 37 [38: 39: 40: 41]cm, ending with RS facing for next row.

Next row (RS): (K1, P1) 3 times, (K2tog, (K3tog) 4 times, K1, (K1, P1) 3 times) 4 [5: 5: 6: 6] times, K1 [0: 1: 1: 1], (P1, K1) 3 [0: 3: 0: 4] times. 61 [66: 73: 79: 87] sts.

Yoke pattern

Next row (WS): (K1, P1) 6 [3: 6: 3: 7] times, K1 [0: 1: 1: 1], (P6, (P1, K1) 3 times) 4 [5: 5: 6: 6] times.

Next row (RS): (K1, P1) 3 times, (K6, (K1, P1) 3 times) 4 [5: 5: 6: 6] times, K1 [0: 1: 1: 1], (P1, K1) 3 [0: 3: 0: 4] times.

These 2 rows set yoke patt.

Work 1 row.

Next row (RS) (Buttonhole row): Patt 2 sts, cast off 2 sts (2 sts to be cast on over these cast off sts on next row), patt to end.

Complete to match left front reversing shapings and working 3 more buttonholes as before to correspond with markers on left front opening edge.

SLEEVES

Using 5½mm (US 9) needles cast on 58 [60: 62: 64: 66] sts.

Row 1 (RS): ★ K1, P1, rep from ★ to end.

Row 2: ★ P1, K1, rep from ★ to end.

These 2 rows form moss st.

Work 2 rows more in moss st.

Row 1 (RS): K2 [3: 4: 5: 6], ★ (P1, K1) 3 times, K6, rep from ★ 3 times more, (P1, K1) 3 times, K2 [3: 4: 5: 6].

Row 2: P2 [3: 4: 5: 6], ★ (K1, P1) 3 times, P6, rep from ★ 3 times

cable and moss st patt panel

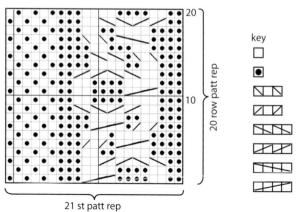

21 st patt rep

key

☐ K on RS, P on WS

▣ P on RS, K on WS

T3F = slip next 2 sts onto cable needle and hold at front of work, P1, then K2 from cable needle

T3B = slip next st onto cable needle and hold at back of work, K2, then P1 from cable needle

T4F = slip next 2 sts onto cable needle and hold at front of work, P2, then K2 from cable needle

T3B = slip next 2 sts onto cable needle and hold at back of work, K2, then P2 from cable needle

C4F = slip next 2 sts onto cable needle and hold at front of work, K2, then K2 from cable needle

C4B = slip next 2 sts onto cable needle and hold at back of work, K2, then K2 from cable needle

more, (K1, P1) 3 times, P2 [3: 4: 5: 6].
These 2 rows form moss st patt.
Cont in moss st patt, shaping sides by inc 1 st at each end of 3rd row, then every foll 6th row to 80 [80: 78: 80: 82] sts, then every foll 8th row to 88 [90: 92: 94: 96] sts, working inc sts in patt.
Cont straight until sleeve meas 43 [44: 45: 45: 45] cm, ending with RS facing for next row.

Shape top
Keeping patt correct, cast off 5 [7: 8: 9: 11] sts at beg of next 2 rows.
78 [76: 76: 76: 74] sts.

Dec 1 st at each end of next 3 rows, then on foll 4 [7: 9: 11: 14] alt rows, then every row to 38 sts.
Cast off 9 sts at beg of next 2 rows. Cast off rem 20 sts.

MAKING UP
Press as described on the information page.
Join shoulder and collar seams. Join side and sleeve seams.
See information page for finishing instructions, setting in sleeves using the set-in method.

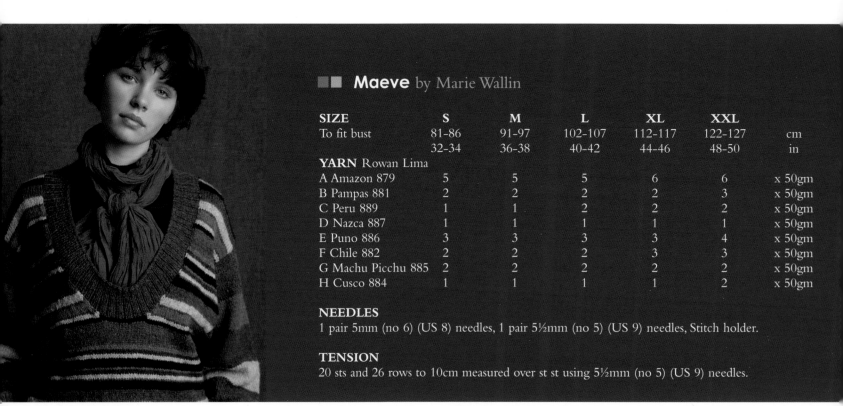

■■ Maeve by Marie Wallin

SIZE	S	M	L	XL	XXL	
To fit bust	81-86	91-97	102-107	112-117	122-127	cm
	32-34	36-38	40-42	44-46	48-50	in
YARN Rowan Lima						
A Amazon 879	5	5	5	6	6	x 50gm
B Pampas 881	2	2	2	2	3	x 50gm
C Peru 889	1	1	2	2	2	x 50gm
D Nazca 887	1	1	1	1	1	x 50gm
E Puno 886	3	3	3	3	4	x 50gm
F Chile 882	2	2	2	3	3	x 50gm
G Machu Picchu 885	2	2	2	2	2	x 50gm
H Cusco 884	1	1	1	1	2	x 50gm

NEEDLES
1 pair 5mm (no 6) (US 8) needles, 1 pair 5½mm (no 5) (US 9) needles, Stitch holder.

TENSION
20 sts and 26 rows to 10cm measured over st st using 5½mm (no 5) (US 9) needles.

Back and front stripe sequence
Rows 1 to 4: Using yarn B.
Rows 5 and 6: Using yarn C.
Rows 7 and 8: Using yarn D.
Rows 9 and 10: Using yarn E.
Rows 11 and 12: Using yarn F.
Rows 13 and 14: Using yarn G.
Rows 15 and 16: Using yarn A.
Rows 17 to 20: Using yarn H.
Rows 21 and 22: Using yarn B.
Rows 23 and 24: Using yarn C.
Row 25: Using yarn G.
Rows 26 to 29: Using yarn E.
Row 30: Using yarn A.
Rows 31 to 34: Using yarn C.
Row 35: Using yarn F.
Rows 36 to 39: Using yarn A.
Row 40: Using yarn G.
Rows 41 to 44: Using yarn B.

Row 45: Using yarn H.
Rows 46 and 47: Using yarn C.
Rows 48 and 49: Using yarn D.
Row 50: Using yarn E.

BACK
Using 5mm (US 8) needles and yarn A cast on 95 [105: 117: 129: 143] sts.
Row 1 (RS): K2 [1: 1: 1: 2], P1, ★ K2, P1, rep from ★ to last 2 [1: 1: 1: 2] sts, K2 [1: 1: 1: 2].
Row 2: P2 [1: 1: 1: 2], K1, ★ P2, K1, rep from ★ to last 2 [1: 1: 1: 2] sts, P2 [1: 1: 1: 2].
These 2 rows form rib.
Work 34 rows more in rib, dec 1 st at centre of last of these rows and ending with RS facing for next row. 94 [104: 116: 128: 142] sts.
Change to 5½mm (US 9) needles. ★★
Beg with a K row and yarn B, cont in st st and stripe sequence as given for back and front, which is repeated throughout, until back meas 42 [43: 44: 45: 46] cm, ending with RS facing for next row.
Place a marker at each end of last row to denote armholes.

Cont straight until back meas 73 [75: 77: 79: 81] cm, ending with RS facing for next row.

Shape shoulders and back neck
Keeping stripe sequence correct, cast off 8 [10: 11: 13: 15] sts at beg of next 2 rows. 78 [84: 94: 102: 112] sts.
Next row (RS): Cast off 8 [10: 12: 14: 16] sts, K until there are 12 [13: 15: 17: 19] sts on right hand needle, turn and leave rem sts on a stitch holder.
Work each side of neck separately.
Next row (WS): Cast off 3 sts, P to end.
Cast off rem 9 [10: 12: 14: 16] sts.
With RS facing, rejoin appropriate yarn to rem sts, cast off centre 38 [38: 40: 40: 42] sts, K to end.
Complete to match first side, reversing shapings.

FRONT
Work as given for back to ★★.
Beg with a K row and yarn B, cont in st st and stripe sequence as given for back and front, which is repeated throughout, until 78 [78: 80: 80: 82] rows less have been worked than on back to shape shoulders, ending with RS facing for next row.

Divide for neck
Next row (RS): K41 [46: 52: 58: 65], turn and leave rem sts on stitch holder.
Work each side of neck separately.
Dec 1 st at neck edge of next 4 rows, then on 10 foll 4th rows, then 2 [2: 3: 3: 4] foll 6th rows. 25 [30: 35: 41: 47] sts.
Work 21 [21: 17: 17: 13] rows, ending with RS facing for next row.
Shape shoulder
Cast off 8 [10: 11: 13: 15] sts at beg of next row, then 8 [10: 12: 14: 16] sts at beg of foll alt row.
Work 1 row.
Cast off rem 9 [10: 12: 14: 16] sts.
With RS facing, rejoin appropriate yarn to rem sts left on a stitch holder, cast off centre 12 sts, K to end.
Complete to match first side, reversing shapings.
Place a marker at each end of row that corresponds with marked row on back to denote armholes.

Sleeve stripe sequence
Rows 1 and 2: Using yarn A.
Rows 3 to 18: Using yarn F.
Rows 19 and 20: Using yarn A
Rows 21 to 36: Using yarn C.
Rows 37 and 38: Using yarn A.
Rows 39 to 54: Using yarn G.
Rows 55 and 56: Using yarn A.
Rows 57 to 72: Using yarn E.

SLEEVES
Using 5mm (US 8) needles and yarn E, cast on 41 [43: 45: 45: 47] sts.
Row 1 (RS): K2 [0: 1: 1: 2], P1, ★ K2, P1, rep from ★ to last 2 [0: 1: 1: 2] sts, K2 [0: 1: 1: 2].

Row 2: P2 [0: 1: 1: 2], K1, ★ P2, K1, rep from ★ to last 2 [0: 1: 1: 2] sts, P2 [0: 1: 1: 2].
These 2 rows form rib.
Cont in rib shaping sides by inc 1 st at each end of 3rd row, then on 5 foll 4th rows working inc sts in rib. 53 [55: 57: 57: 59] sts.
Work 1 row.
Change to 5½mm (US 9) needles and yarn A.
Next row (RS): K2 [3: 4: 4: 5], M1, (K4, M1) 12 times, K3 [4: 5: 5: 6]. 66 [68: 70: 70: 72] sts.
Beg with a P row and row 2 of stripe sequence which is repeated throughout, cont in st st shaping sides by inc 1 st at each end of 4th row, then on every foll alt row to 82 [82: 82: 82: 84] sts, then every foll 4th row to 116 [118: 120: 120: 122] sts.
Cont straight until sleeve meas 47 [48: 49: 49: 49] cm, ending with RS facing for next row.
Cast off.

MAKING UP
Press as described on the information page.
Join right shoulder seam.
Neck edging
With RS facing and using 5mm (US 8) needles and yarn A, pick up and knit 64 [64: 66: 66: 68] sts down left side of neck, 12 sts from front neck, 64 [64: 66: 66: 68] sts up right side of neck and 44 [44: 46: 46: 48] sts from back neck. 184 [184: 190: 190: 196] sts.
Next row (WS): K1, ★ P2, K1, rep from ★ to end.
Next row: P1 ★ K2, P1, rep from ★ to end.
These 2 rows form rib.
Work 14 rows more in rib.
Cast off in rib.
Join left shoulder seam and neck edging. Join cast off edges of sleeves to armholes between markers on back and front.
See information page for finishing instructions.

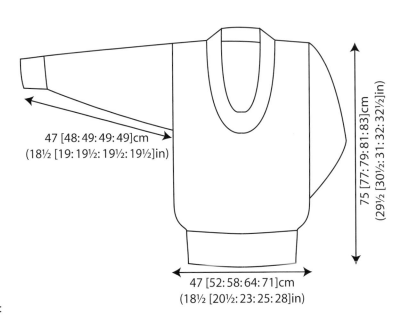

47 [48: 49: 49: 49]cm
(18½ [19: 19½: 19½: 19½]in)

75 [77: 79: 81: 83]cm
(29½ [30½: 31: 32: 32½]in)

47 [52: 58: 64: 71]cm
(18½ [20½: 23: 25: 28]in)

Nathan by Marie Wallin

SIZE	S	M	L	XL	XXL	2XL	
To fit chest							
	102	107	112	117	122	127	cm
	40	42	44	46	48	50	in

YARN
Rowan Lima

	18	19	20	22	23	24	x 50gm

(photographed in Amazon 879)

NEEDLES
1 pair 5mm (no 6) (US 8) needles, 1 pair 5½mm (no 5) (US 9) needles, Cable needle.

TENSION
26 sts and 26 rows to 10cm measured over patt using 5½mm (no5) (US 9) needles .

SPECIAL ABBREVIATIONS

C4F=slip next 2 sts onto a cable needle and hold at front of work, K2, then K2 from cable needle; **C4B**=slip next 2 sts onto a cable needle and hold at back of work, K2, then K2 from cable needle; **CN**=cable needle.

NOTE: When counting sts always count cable panel as 49 sts.

CABLE PANEL (49 sts)
Row 1 (RS): (P2, K4) 4 times, P1, (K4, P2) 4 times.
Row 2: (K2, P4) 4 times, K1, (P4, K2) 4 times.
Row 3: (P2, C4F, P2, K4) twice, P1, (K4, P2, C4B, P2) twice.
Row 4: As row 2.
Row 5: As row 1.
Row 6: As row 2.
Row 7: P2, C4F, P2, K4, P2, C4F, P2, sl next 5 sts onto CN and hold at front of work, K4, then sl P st from CN back to left needle and P, K4 from CN, P2, C4B, P2, K4, P2, C4B, P2.
Row 8: As row 2.
Row 9: P2, K4, P2, ★ M1, (K4, P2) twice, K4, M1, ★ P1, rep from ★ to ★ once more, P2, K4, P2. 53 sts.
Row 10: K2, P4, ★ K3, P4, (K2, P4) twice, rep from ★ once more, K3, P4, K2.
Row 11: P2, C4F, P3, M1, K4, P2tog, C4F, P2tog, K4, M1, P3, M1, K4, P2tog, C4B, P2tog, K4, M1, P3, C4B, P2.
Row 12: K2, P4, K4, ★ (P4, K1) twice, P4 ★, K5, rep from ★ to ★ once more, K4, P4, K2.
Row 13: P2, K4, P4, ★ M1, K3, sl 1, K1, psso, K4, K2tog, K3, M1, ★ P5, rep from ★ to ★ once more, P4, K4, P2.
Row 14: K2, P4, K5, P12, K7, P12, K5, P4, K2.
Row 15: P2, C4F, P5, M1, K4, C4F, K4, M1, P7, M1, K4, C4B, K4, M1, P5, C4B, P2. 57 sts.
Row 16: K2, P4, K6, P12, K9, P12, K6, P4, K2.
Row 17: P2, K4, P6, sl next 8 sts onto CN and hold at back of work, K4, sl 2nd 4 sts from CN back onto left needle and K, K4 from CN, P9, sl next 8 sts onto CN and hold at front of work, K4, sl 2nd 4 sts from CN back onto left needle and K, K4 from CN, P6, K4, P2.
Row 18: As row 16.
Row 19: P2, C4F, P4, P2tog, K4, C4F, K4, P2tog, P5, P2tog, K4, C4B, K4, P2tog, P4, C4B, P2. 53 sts.
Row 20: As row 14.
Row 21: P2, K4, P3, ★ P2tog, (K4, M1) twice, K4, P2tog, P3, rep from ★ once more, K4, P2.
Row 22: As row 12.
Row 23 : P2, C4F, P2, P2tog, K4, M1, P1, C4F, P1, M1, K4, P2tog, P1, P2tog, K4, M1, P1, C4B, P1, M1, K4, P2tog, P2, C4B, P2.
Row 24: As row 10.
Row 25: P2, K4, P1, P2tog, ★ (K4, P2) twice, K4 ★, P3tog, rep from ★ to ★ once more, P2tog, P1, K4, P2. 49 sts.
Row 26: As row 2.
Row 27: As row 7.
Row 28: As row 2.
These 28 rows form cable panel.

BACK AND FRONT (both alike)
Using 5mm (US 8) needles and cast on 145 [153: 161: 169: 177: 185] sts.
Row 1 (RS):K0 [4: 2: 0: 4: 2], (P2, K4) 12 [12: 13: 14: 14: 15] times, P1, (K4, P2) 12 [12: 13: 14: 14: 15] times, K0 [4: 2: 0: 4: 2].
Row 2: P0 [4: 2: 0: 4: 2], (K2, P4) 12 [12: 13: 14: 14: 15] times, K1, (P4, K2) 12 [12: 13: 14: 14: 15] times, P0 [4: 2: 0: 4: 2].
These 2 rows form rib.
Work 16 rows more in rib, ending with RS facing for next row.
Change to 5½mm (US 9) needles.
Row 1 (RS) : K0 [4: 2: 0: 4: 2], P0 [0: 2: 0: 0: 2], K0 [0: 4: 0: 0: 4], (P2, K4) 8 [8: 8: 10: 10: 10] times, work next 49 sts as row 1 of cable panel, (K4, P2) 8 [8: 8: 10: 10: 10] times, K0 [0: 4: 0: 0: 4], P0 [0: 2: 0:

0: 2], K0 [4: 2: 0: 4: 2].

Row 2 : P0 [4: 2: 0: 4: 2], K0 [0: 2: 0: 0: 2], P0 [0: 4: 0: 0: 4], (K2, P4) 8 [8: 8: 10: 10: 10] times, work next 49 sts as row 2 of cable panel, (P4, K2) 8 [8: 8: 10: 10: 10] times, P0 [0: 4: 0: 0: 4], K0 [0: 2: 0: 0: 2], P0 [4: 2: 0: 4: 2].

Row 3 : K0 [4: 2: 0: 4: 2], P0 [0: 2: 0: 0: 2], K0 [0: 4: 0: 0: 4], (P2, C4F, P2, K4) 4 [4: 4: 5: 5: 5] times, work next 49 sts as row 3 of cable panel, (K4, P2, C4B, P2) 4 [4: 4: 5: 5: 5] times, K0 [0: 4: 0: 0: 4], P0 [0: 2: 0: 0: 2], K0 [4: 2: 0: 4: 2].

Row 4 : P0 [4: 2: 0: 4: 2], K0 [0: 2: 0: 0: 2], P0 [0: 4: 0: 0: 4], (K2, P4) 8 [8: 8: 10: 10: 10] times, work next 49 sts as row 4 of cable panel, (P4, K2) 8 [8: 8: 10: 10: 10] times, P0 [0: 4: 0: 0: 4], K0 [0: 2: 0: 0: 2], P0 [4: 2: 0: 4: 2].

These 4 rows set patt – cable panel on centre 49 sts, with rib and cable either side.

Cont in patt as set until work meas 38 [39: 38: 39: 38: 39] cm, ending with RS facing for next row.

Shape armholes

Dec 1 st at each end of next 5 [5: 3: 1: 1: 1] rows, then on 4 [3: 3: 4: 3: 2] foll alt rows. 127 [137: 149: 159: 169: 179] sts.
Cont straight until armholes meas 27 [28: 29: 30: 31: 32] cm, ending with RS facing for next row.

Shape shoulders

Cast off 11 [12: 14: 16: 17: 18] sts at beg of next 2 rows, then 11 [13: 14: 16: 17: 19] sts at beg of foll 2 rows and 11 [13: 15: 16: 17: 19] sts at beg of foll 2 rows. 61 [61: 63: 63: 67: 67] sts.

Funnel neck

Dec 1 st at each end of 3rd row, then foll 4th row.
57 [57: 59: 59: 63: 63] sts.
Work 3 rows, ending with RS facing for next row.
Cast off.

SLEEVES

Using 5mm (US 8) needles cast on 61 [63: 65: 67: 71: 73] sts.
Row 1 (RS): P0 [0: 0: 0: 1: 0], K0 [1: 2: 3: 4: 0], (P2, K4) 5 [5: 5: 5: 5: 6] times, P1, (K4, P2) 5 [5: 5: 5: 5: 6] times, K0 [1: 2: 3: 4: 0], P0 [0: 0: 0: 1: 0].
Row 2: K0 [0: 0: 0: 1: 0], P0 [1: 2: 3: 4: 0], (K2, P4) 5 [5: 5: 5: 5: 6] times, K1, (P4, K2) 5 [5: 5: 5: 5: 6] times, P0 [1: 2: 3: 4: 0], K0 [0: 0: 0: 1: 0].
These 2 rows form rib.
Work 16 rows more in rib, ending with RS facing for next row.
Change to 5½mm (US 9) needles.
Row 1 (RS): P0 [0: 0: 0: 1: 0], K0 [1: 2: 3: 4: 0], (P2, K4) 1 [1: 1: 1: 1: 2] times, work next 49 sts as row 1 of cable panel, (K4, P2) 1 [1: 1: 1: 1: 2] times, K0 [1: 2: 3: 4: 0], P0 [0: 0: 0: 1: 0].
Row 2 : K0 [0: 0: 0: 1: 0], P0 [1: 2: 3: 4: 0], (K2, P4) 1 [1: 1: 1: 1: 2] times, work next 49 sts as row 2 of cable panel, (P4, K2) 1 [1: 1: 1: 1: 2] times, P0 [1: 2: 3: 4: 0], K0 [0: 0: 0: 1: 0].
These 2 rows set patt – cable panel on centre 49 sts, with rib and cable either side.
Cont in patt as set shaping sides by inc 1 st at each end of 3rd row, then on every foll alt row to 93 [89: 87: 83: 83: 79] sts, then every foll 4th row to 131 [133: 135: 137: 141: 143] sts, working

inc sts in rib and cable patt.
Cont straight until sleeve meas 53 [55: 57: 59: 61: 63] cm, ending with RS facing for next row.

Shape top

Dec 1 st at each end of next 16 [18: 20: 22: 24: 26] rows.
99 [97: 95: 93: 93: 91] sts.
Cast off 33 [32: 31: 30: 30: 29] sts at beg of next 2 rows.
Cast off rem 33 sts.

MAKING UP

Press as described on the information page.
Join right shoulder and funnel neck seam.

Neck edging

With RS facing and using 5mm (US 8) needles pick up and knit 114 [114: 118: 118: 126: 126] sts all around neck edge.
Cast off.
Join left shoulder and funnel neck seam.
See information page for finishing instructions, setting in sleeves using the shallow set-in method.

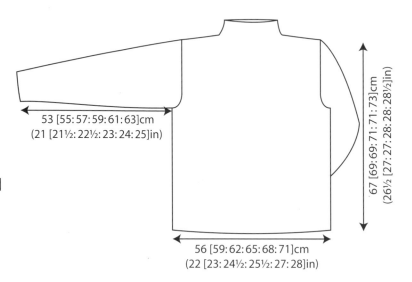

53 [55: 57: 59: 61: 63]cm
(21 [21½: 22½: 23: 24: 25]in)

67 [69: 69: 71: 71: 73]cm
(26½ [27: 27: 28: 28: 28½]in)

56 [59: 62: 65: 68: 71]cm
(22 [23: 24½: 25½: 27: 28]in)

Quinn by Marie Wallin

SIZE	S	M	L	XL	XXL	2XL	
To fit chest							
	102	107	112	117	122	127	cm
	40	42	44	46	48	50	in
YARN							
Rowan Lima	30	32	34	37	39	42	x 50gm
(photographed in Nazca 887)							

NEEDLES

1 pair 7mm (no 2) (US 10½) needles, 1 pair 8mm (no 0) (US 11) needles, Stitch holder, Cable needle.

EXTRAS

5 x BN11372 toggle fasteners from Bedecked.

TENSION

20 sts and 19 rows to 10 cm measured over patt using 8mm (no 0) (US 11) needles and **2 ends of yarn**.

SPECIAL ABBREVIATIONS

C6B=slip next 3 sts onto a cable needle and hold at back of work, K3, then K3 from cable needle; **C6F**=slip next 3 sts onto a cable needle and hold at front of work, K3, then K3 from cable needle; **T4F**=slip next 3 sts onto a cable needle and hold at front of work, P1, then K3 from cable needle; **T4B**=slip next st onto a cable needle and hold at back of work, K3, then P1 from cable needle; **C4B**=slip next 2 sts onto a cable needle and hold at back of work, K2, then K2 from cable needle; **C4F**=slip next 2 sts onto a cable needle and hold at front of work, K2, then K2 from cable needle.

BACK

Using 7mm (US 10½) needles and **2 ends of yarn** cast on 116 [122: 128: 134: 140: 146] sts.
Beg and ending rows as indicated, work 11 rows in rib pattern beg with row 1 of chart A, ending with **WS** facing for next row.
Change to 8mm (US 11) needles.
Now work in cable patt from chart A, beg with row 12 which is a **WS** row and repeating rows 12 to 35, as follows:
Cont in patt until back meas 37 [38: 37: 38: 37: 38] cm, ending with RS facing for next row.

Shape armholes

Keeping patt correct cast off 3 [3: 2: 2: 2: 1] sts at beg of next 2 rows.
110 [116: 124: 130: 136: 144] sts.
Dec 1 st at each end of next 5 [3: 3: 3: 3: 3] rows, then on foll 1 [2: 2: 1: -: -] alt rows. 98 [106: 114: 122: 130: 138] sts.
Work 9 [9: 9: 11: 13: 13] rows, ending with RS facing for next row.

Yoke patt

Next Row (RS): Purl.
Next row: Knit.
Next row: Purl.
Now work in yoke patt from chart B beg with row 1 which is a **WS** row and repeating rows 1 to 8, as folls:
Cont straight until armholes meas 27 [28: 29: 30: 31: 32] cm,

ending with RS facing for next row.

Shape shoulders and back neck

Cast off 10 [11: 12: 13: 14: 16] sts at beg of next 2 rows.
78 [84: 90: 96: 102: 106] sts.
Next row (RS): Cast off 10 [11: 12: 14: 15: 16] sts, patt until there are 13 [15: 16: 17: 18: 19] sts on right hand needle, turn and leave rem sts on a stitch holder.
Work each side of neck separately.
Next row (WS): Cast off 3 sts, P to end.
Cast off rem 10 [12: 13: 14: 15: 16] sts.
With RS facing, rejoin yarn to rem sts, cast off centre 32 [32: 34: 34: 36: 36] sts, patt to end.
Complete to match first side reversing shapings.

LEFT FRONT

Using 7mm (US 10½) needles and **2 ends of yarn** cast on 69 [72: 75: 78: 81: 84] sts.
Row 1 (RS): Work 48 [51: 54: 57: 60: 63] sts in rib patt beg with row 1 of chart A, (K3, P3) 3 times, K3.
Row 2: P3, (K3, P3) 3 times, work 48 [51: 54: 57: 60: 63] sts from row 2 of chart.
These 2 rows set the sts, chart rib patt and 21 sts in 3 x 3 rib for front edging.
Work 9 rows more in patt as set, ending with **WS** facing for next row.
Change to 8mm (US 11) needles.
Keeping 21 sts for front edging correct in rib patt as set, work rem 48 [51: 54: 57: 60: 63] sts in cable patt from chart A beg with row 12 which is a **WS** row and repeating rows 12 to 35 as folls:
Cont in patt until left front matches back to shape armholes, ending with RS facing for next row.

Shape armhole

Keeping patt correct cast off 3 [3: 2: 2: 2: 1] sts at beg of next row.
66 [69: 73: 76: 79: 83] sts.
Work 1 row.
Dec 1 st at armhole edge of next 5 [3: 3: 3: 3: 3] rows, then on

Chart B

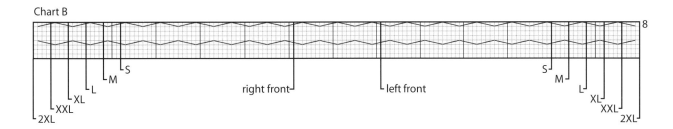

8

S
M
L
XL
XXL
2XL

right front

left front

S
M
L
XL
XXL
2XL

Chart A

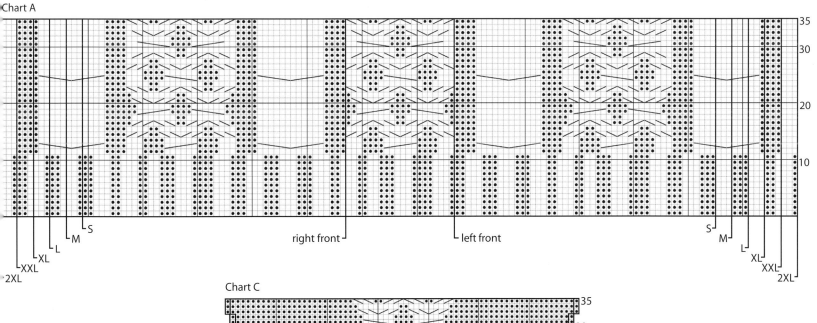

35
30

20

10

S
M
L
XL
XXL
2XL

right front

left front

S
M
L
XL
XXL
2XL

Chart C

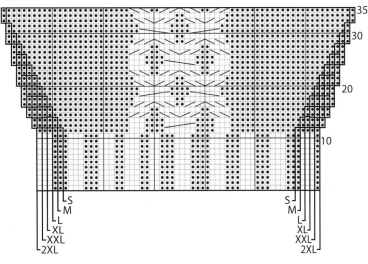

35
30

20

10

S
M
L
XL
XXL
2XL

S
M
L
XL
XXL
2XL

key

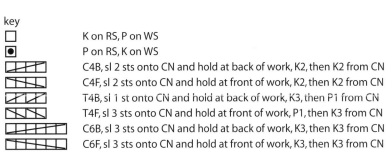

☐   K on RS, P on WS

⊙   P on RS, K on WS

C4B, sl 2 sts onto CN and hold at back of work, K2, then K2 from CN

C4F, sl 2 sts onto CN and hold at front of work, K2, then K2 from CN

T4B, sl 1 st onto CN and hold at back of work, K3, then P1 from CN

T4F, sl 3 sts onto CN and hold at front of work, P1, then K3 from CN

C6B, sl 3 sts onto CN and hold at back of work, K3, then K3 from CN

C6F, sl 3 sts onto CN and hold at front of work, K3, then K3 from CN foll 1 [2: 2: 1: -: -] alt rows. 60 [64: 68: 72: 76: 80] sts.

Work 9 [9: 9: 11: 13: 13] rows, ending with RS facing for next row.

Yoke patt

Next row (RS): P39 [43: 47: 51: 55: 59], (K3, P3) 3 times, K3.

Next row: P3, (K3, P3) 3 times, K to end.

Next row: P39 [43: 47: 51: 55: 59], (K3, P3) 3 times, K3.

Now work in yoke patt from chart B, beg with row 1 which is a **WS** row and repeating rows 1 to 8, as folls:

Cont straight until 5 [5: 7: 7: 9: 9] rows less have been worked than on back to shape shoulders, ending with **WS** facing for next row.

Shape neck

Next row (WS): Keeping patt correct cast off 27 sts, patt to end. 33 [37: 41: 45: 49: 53] sts.

Dec 1 st at neck edge of next 3 [3: 4: 4: 5: 5] rows. 30 [34: 37: 41: 44: 48] sts.

Work 1 [1: 2: 2: 3: 3] rows, ending with RS facing for next row.

Shape shoulder

Cast off 10 [11: 12: 13: 14: 16] sts at beg of next row, then 10 [11: 12: 14: 15: 16] sts at beg of foll alt row.

Work 1 row.

Cast off rem 10 [12: 13: 14: 15: 16] sts.

RIGHT FRONT

Using 7mm (US 10½) needles and **2 ends of yarn** cast on 69 [72: 75: 78: 81: 84] sts.

Row 1 RS): K3, (P3, K3) 3 times, work 48 [51: 54: 57: 60: 63] sts in rib patt beg with row 1 of chart A.

Row 2: Work 48 [51: 54: 57: 60: 63] sts from row 2 of chart, (P3, K3) 3 times, P3.

These 2 rows set the sts, 21 sts in 3 x 3 rib for front edging and chart rib patt.

Work as given for left front reversing shapings.

SLEEVES

Using 7mm (US 10½) needles and **2 ends of yarn** cast on 46 [48: 50: 52: 54: 56] sts.

Beg and ending rows as indicated work 11 rows in rib pattern beg

with row 1 of chart C, ending with **WS** facing for next row.

Change to 8mm (US 11) needles.

Now work in cable patt with rev st st either side from chart C beg with row 12 which is a **WS** row and repeating rows 12 to 35, as folls:

Cont in patt shaping sides by inc 1 st at each end of 2nd row then on every foll alt row to 68 [66: 64: 62: 60: 60] sts, then every foll 4th row to 98 [100: 102: 104: 106: 108] sts, working inc sts in rev st st.

Cont straight until sleeve meas 53 [55: 57: 59: 61: 63] cm, ending with RS facing for next row.

Shape top

Keeping patt correct cast off 3 [3: 2: 2: 2: 1] sts at beg of next 2 rows. 92 [94: 98: 100: 102: 106] sts.

Dec 1 st at each end of next 10 [12: 14: 16: 18: 20] rows. 72 [70: 70: 68: 66: 66] sts.

Cast off 16 [15: 15: 14: 13: 13] sts at beg of next 2 rows.

Cast off rem 40 sts.

MAKING UP

Press as described on the information page.

Join shoulder seams.

Collar

Using 7mm (US 10½) needles and **2 ends of yarn**, cast on 105 [105: 111: 111: 117: 117] sts.

Next row (RS): ★ K3, P3, rep from ★ to last 3 sts, K3.

Next row: P3, ★ K3, P3, rep from ★ to end.

These 2 rows form 3x3 rib.

Work 16 rows more in rib, ending with RS facing for next row.

Cast off 3 sts in rib at beg of next 12 rows.

Cast off rem 69 [69: 75: 75: 81: 81] sts in rib.

Join cast off edge of collar to garment placing row end edges of collar 5 cm in from front edges.

Toggle fasteners (make 3)

Using yarn double and 8mm crochet hook work length of ch 14cm long. Using photograph as a guide attach to garment with toggles on opposite side.

See information page for finishing instructions, setting in sleeves using the shallow set-in method.

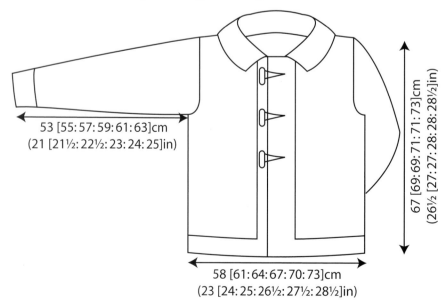

53 [55: 57: 59: 61: 63]cm
(21 [21½: 22½: 23: 24: 25]in)

67 [69: 69: 71: 71: 73]cm
(26½ [27: 27: 28: 28: 28½]in)

58 [61: 64: 67: 70: 73]cm
(23 [24: 25: 26½: 27½: 28½]in)

Tallulah by Sarah Hatton

	S	M	L	XL	XXL	
To fit bust						
	81–86	91–96	102–107	112–117	122–127	cm
	32–34	36–38	40–42	44–46	48–50	in

YARN

Rowan Lima	13	14	15	17	18	x 50gm

(photographed in Amazon 879)

NEEDLES

1 pair 5mm (no 6) (US 8), 1 pair 5½mm (no 5) (US 9) needles, Stitch holders.

EXTRAS

6 x BN1369 (50mm) buttons from Bedecked.

TENSION

20 sts and 26 rows to 10 cm measured over st st using 5½mm (no 5) (US 9) needles.

SPECIAL ABBREVIATIONS

MB= (K1, P1, K1) into next st, turn, P3, turn, K3, turn, P3, turn, K3tog; **KB1**=K into back of st; **PB1**= P into back of st; **T2F**= Slip 1 st onto cable needle and hold at front of work, P1, then K1 from cable needle; **T2B**= Slip 1 st onto cable needle and hold at back of work, K1, then P1 from cable needle; **T2FW**= Slip 1 st onto cable needle and hold at front of work, P1, then K1 from cable needle on WS row; **T2BW**= Slip 1 st onto cable needle and hold at back of work, K1, then P1 from cable needle on WS row; **M1P**=pick up yarn between next and last st and p into back to make a st; **C4F**=slip next 2 sts onto a cable needle and hold at front of work, K2, then K2 from cable needle; **C4B**= slip next 2 sts onto a cable needle and hold at back of work, K2, then K2 from cable needle; **T4B**= slip next 2 sts onto a cable needle and hold at back of work, K2, then P2 from cable needle; **T4F**= slip next 2 sts onto a cable needle and hold at front of work, P2, then P2 from cable needle; **T3B**= slip next st onto a cable needle and hold at back of work, K2, then K1 from cable needle; **T3F**= slip next 2 sts onto a cable needle and hold at front of work, K1, then K2 from cable needle

CABLE PANEL A (27 sts)

Row 1 (RS): P2, C2B, C2F, P7, MB, P7, C2B, C2F, P2.
Row 2: K2, P4, K7, PB1, K7, P4, K2.
Row 3: P2, C2F, C2B, P4, MB, P2, KB1, P2, MB, P4, C2F, C2B, P2.
Row 4: K2, P4, K4, (PB1, K2) 3 times, K2, P4, K2.
Row 5: P2, C2B, C2F, P2, MB, P1, T2F, P1, KB1, P1, T2B, P1, MB, P2, C2B, C2F, P2.
Row 6: K2, P4, (K2, PB1) twice, (K1, PB1) twice, K2, PB1, K2, P4, K2.
Row 7: P2, C2F, C2B, P2 T2F, P1, T2F, KB1, T2B, P1, T2B, P2, C2F, C2B, P2.
Row 8: K2, P4, K3, T2BW, K1, (PB1) 3 times, K1, T2FW, K3, P4, K2.

Row 9: P2, C2B, C2F, P4, T2F, M1P, Sl 1, K2tog, psso, M1P, T2B, P4, C2B, C2F, P2.
Row 10: K2, P4, K5, T2BW, PB1, T2FW, K5, P4, K2.
Row 11: P2, C2F, C2B, P6, M1P, Sl 1, K2tog, psso, M1P, P6, C2F, C2B, P2.
Row 12: K2, P4, K7, PB1, K7, P4, K2.
Row 13: P2, C2B, C2F, P15, C2B, C2F, P2.
Row 14: K2, P4, K15, P4, K2.
Row 15: P2, C2F, C2B, P15, C2F, C2B, P2.
Row 16: As row 14.
These 16 rows form patt.

CABLE PANEL B (14 sts)

Row 1 (RS): P3, K8, P3.
Row 2: K3, P8, K3.
Row 3: P3, C4B, C4F, P3.
Row 4: As row 2.
Rows 5 and 6: As 1st and 2nd rows.
Row 7: P3, T4B, T4F, P3.
Row 8: K3, P2, K4, P2, K3.
Row 9: P2, T3B, P4, T3F, P2.
Row 10: K2, P2, K6, P2, K2.
Row 11: P2, K2, P6, K2, P2.
Row 12: As row 10.
Row 13: P2, T3F, P4, T3B, P2.
Row 14: As row 8.
Row 15: P3, C4F, C4B, P3.
Row 16: K3, P8, K3.
These 16 rows form patt.

BACK

Using 5½mm (US 9) needles cast on 94 [102: 114: 126: 142] sts.
Work 2 rows in garter st, ending with RS facing for next row.
Row 1 (RS): Purl.
Row 2: K1, ★ (K1, P1, K1) into next st, P3tog, rep from ★ to last

st, K1.

Row 3: Purl.

Row 4: K1, ★ P3tog, (K1, P1, K1) into next st, rep from ★ to last st, K1.

These 4 rows form patt.

Work 16 rows more in patt, ending with RS facing for next row. ★★

Work 2 rows in g st, dec 2 [0: 0: 0: 2] sts evenly across last of these rows. 92 [102: 114: 126: 140] sts.

Beg with a K row, cont in st st until back meas 34 [35: 36: 37: 38]cm, ending with RS facing for next row.

Shape armholes

Cast off 4 [4: 5: 7: 9] sts at beg of next 2 rows. 84 [94: 104: 112: 122] sts.

Dec 1 st at each end of next 3 [5: 7: 9: 9] rows, then on 5 [6: 6: 6: 7] alt rows. 68 [72: 78: 82: 90] sts.

Cont straight until armholes meas 21 [22: 23: 24: 25] cm, ending with RS facing for next row.

Shape shoulders

Cast off 5 [5: 6: 7: 8] sts at beg of next 2 rows. 58 [62: 66: 68: 74] sts.

Next row (RS): Cast off 5 [6: 6: 7: 8] sts, K until there are 8 [9: 10: 10: 11] sts on right needle, turn and leave rem sts on a stitch holder.

Work each side of neck separately.

Next row (WS): Cast off 3 sts, P to end.

Cast off rem 5 [6: 7: 7: 8] sts.

With RS facing rejoin yarn to rem sts, cast off centre 32 [32: 34: 34: 36] sts, K to end.

Complete to match first side reversing shapings.

LEFT FRONT

Using 5½mm (US 9) needles cast on 46 [54: 58: 66: 70] sts.

Work as given for back to ★★.

Work 2 rows in g st, dec 0 [3: 1: 3: 0] sts evenly across last of these rows. 46 [51: 57: 63: 70] sts.

Place pocket

Next row (RS): K10 [15: 21: 27: 34], leave rem 36 sts on a stitch holder, cast on 36 sts for pocket lining and turn.

Beg with a P row, work 32 rows in st st on these 46 [51: 57: 63: 70] sts only, ending with **WS** facing for next row.

Next row (WS): Cast off 36 sts, P to end.

Leave rem 10 [15: 21: 27: 34] sts on a second st holder **do not break off yarn**.

With RS facing, working on 36 sts left on first st holder cont as folls:

Row 1 (RS): K9, work 27 sts from cable panel A beg with row 1.

This row sets patt – st st with 16 rows of cable panel A which are repeated throughout.

Work 33 rows in patt as set, ending with RS facing for next row. Break off yarn.

Next row (RS): K10 [15: 21: 27: 34] sts from second st holder, then patt across 36 sts on needle. 46 [51: 57: 63: 70] sts.

Cont straight in patt until left front matches back to shape armholes, ending with RS facing for next row.

Shape armhole

Next row (RS): Keeping patt correct, cast off 4 [4: 5: 7: 9] sts, patt to end. 42 [47: 52: 56: 61] sts.

Work 1 row.

Dec 1 st at armhole in next 3 [5: 7: 9: 9] rows, then on foll 5 [6: 6: 6: 7] alt rows. 34 [36: 39: 41: 45] sts.

Cont straight until 19 [19: 21: 21: 25] rows less have been worked than on back to shape shoulders, ending with **WS** facing for next row.

Shape neck

Next row (WS): Keeping patt correct, cast off 9 sts, patt to end. 25 [27: 30: 32: 36] sts.

Dec 1 st at neck edge of next 5 rows, then on foll 5 [5: 6: 6: 7] alt rows. 15 [17: 19: 21: 24] sts.

Work 3 [3: 3: 3: 5] rows, ending with RS facing for next row.

Shape shoulder

Cast off 5 [5: 6: 7: 8] sts at beg of next row, then 5 [6: 6: 7: 8] at beg of foll alt row.

Work 1 row.

Cast off rem 5 [6: 7: 7: 8] sts.

RIGHT FRONT

Using 5½mm (US 9) needles cast on 46 [54: 58: 66: 70] sts.

Work as given for back to ★★.

Work 2 rows in g st, dec 0 [3: 1: 3: 0] sts evenly across last of these rows. 46 [51: 57: 63: 70] sts.

Place pocket

Next row (RS): Work 27 sts from cable panel A beg with row 1, K9, leave rem 10 [15: 21: 27: 34] sts on a stitch holder.

Work 33 rows in patt as set, ending with RS facing for next row. Leave these sts on a second st holder **do not break off yarn**.

With RS facing, working on 10 [15: 21: 27: 34] sts left on first st holder cont as folls:

Cast on 36 sts, K to end.

Work 32 rows more in st st, ending with RS facing for next row.

Next row (RS): Cast off 36 sts, K to end.

Work 1 row. Break off yarn.

Next Row (RS): Patt across 36 sts from second st holder then 10 [15: 21: 27: 34] sts rem on needle. 46 [51: 57: 63: 70] sts.

Complete as given for left front, reversing shapings.

SLEEVES

Using 5½mm (US 9) needles cast on 46 [46: 50: 50: 54] sts.

Work 2 rows in g st.

Work 14 rows in patt as given for back, ending with RS facing for next row.

Work 2 rows in g st, dec 2 [-: 2: -: 2] sts evenly across last of these rows. 44 [46: 48: 50: 52] sts.

Row 1 (RS): K15 [16: 17: 18: 19], work next 14 sts from row 1 of cable panel B, K15 [16: 17: 18: 18].

This row sets patt – centre 14 sts from cable panel B with st st either side.

Cont in patt as set rep 16 rows of chart, shaping sides by inc 1 st at each end of 2nd row, then on every foll 6th row to 56 [56: 56:

58: 60] sts, then every foll 8th row to 70 [72: 74: 76: 78] sts, working inc sts in st st.

Cont straight until sleeve meas 46 [47: 48: 48: 48] cm, ending with RS facing for next row.

Shape top

Keeping patt correct, cast off 4 [4: 5: 7: 9] sts at beg of next 2 rows. 62 [64: 64: 62: 60] sts.

Dec 1 st at each end of next 3 rows, then on 10 [11: 13: 13: 16] foll alt rows, then every row to 26 [26: 26: 20: 20] sts.

Cast off 7 [7: 7: 5: 5] sts at beg of next 2 rows.

Cast off rem 12 [12: 12: 10: 10] sts.

MAKING UP

Press as described on the information page.

Join shoulder seams.

Hood

With RS facing and using 5½mm (US 9) needles, beg and ending at front slope shaping, pick up and knit 29 [29: 30: 30: 31] sts up right side of neck, 38 [38: 39: 39: 40] sts from back neck and 29 [29: 30: 30: 31] sts down left side of neck. 96 [96: 99: 99: 102] sts.

Beg with a P row cont in st st until hood meas 24cm, ending with RS facing for next row.

Cast off 32 [32: 33: 33: 34] sts at beg of next 2 rows. 32 [32: 33: 33: 34] sts.

Cont on these rem sts until hood meas 16 [16: 16.5: 16.5: 17] cm from cast off sts, ending with RS facing for next row. Cast off.

Join row end edges of top section of hood to cast off edges.

With RS facing and using 5mm (US 8) needles pick up and knit 48 sts from right side of hood, 31 [31: 31: 31: 33] sts across top and 48 sts down left side. 127 [127: 127: 127: 129] sts.

Row 1 (WS): P1, ★ K1, P1, rep from ★ to end.

Row 2 (RS): ★ K1, P1, rep from ★ to last st, K1.

These 2 rows form rib.

Work 8 rows more in rib. Cast off in rib.

Join row end edges of rib to neck edges.

Join side and sleeve seams.

Right front edging

With RS facing and using 5mm (US 8) needles, pick up and knit 95 [99: 101: 105: 107] sts evenly along right front edge.

Work 4 rows in rib as given for hood, ending with **WS** facing for next row.

Next row (RS) (buttonhole row): Rib 4 [3: 2: 4: 2], cast off 2 sts (2 sts to be cast on over these cast off sts on foll row), (rib 14 [15: 16: 16: 17], cast off 2 sts) 5 times, rib 3 [3: 1: 3: 2].

Work 5 rows more in rib.

Cast off in rib.

Left front edging

Work as given for right front edging omitting buttonholes.

Slip stitch pocket linings to inside of garment.

Pocket edgings (both alike)

With RS facing and using 5mm (US 8) needles, pick up and knit 27 sts evenly along pocket edge.

Work 6 rows in rib as given for left front edging. Cast off in rib.

Slip stitch row end edges of pocket edgings flat to garment

See information page for finishing instructions, setting in sleeve using the set-in method.

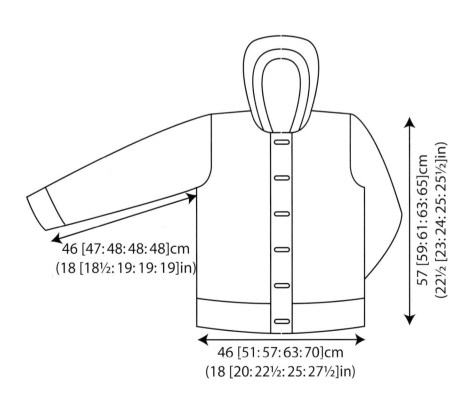

46 [47: 48: 48: 48]cm
(18 [18½: 19: 19: 19]in)

57 [59: 61: 63: 65]cm
(22½ [23: 24: 25: 25½]in)

46 [51: 57: 63: 70]cm
(18 [20: 22½: 25: 27½]in)

Rafferty by Sarah Hatton

SIZE	S	M	L	XL	XXL	2XL	
To fit chest							
	102	107	112	117	122	127	cm
	40	42	44	46	48	50	in

YARN

Rowan Lima

	13	14	15	16	17	18	x 50gm

(photographed in Lima 888)

NEEDLES

1 pair 5mm (no 6) (US 8) needles, 1 pair 5½mm (no 5) (US 9) needles, Stitch holder, Cable needle.

TENSION

20 sts and 26 rows to 10 cm measured over st st using 5½mm (no 5) (US 9) needles .

SPECIAL ABBREVIATIONS

T5B=slip next 2 sts onto cable needle and hold at back of work, K1, P1, K1, then P1, K1 from cable needle

BACK

Using 5mm (US 8) needles cast on 115 [121: 127: 133: 139: 145] sts.
Row 1 (RS): ★ K1, P1, rep from ★ to last st, K1.
Row 2: P1, ★ K1, P1, rep from ★ to end.
These 2 rows form rib.
Work 16 rows more in rib, ending with RS facing for next row.
Change to 5½mm (US 9) needles. ★★
Beg with a P row, cont in rev st st until back meas 41 [42: 41: 42: 41: 42] cm, ending with RS facing for next row.
Shape armholes
Cast off 4 [3: 2: 2: 2: 1] sts at beg of next 2 rows.
107 [115: 123: 129: 135: 143] sts.
Next row (RS): P2, P2tog, P to last 4 sts, P2togtbl, P2.
Next row: K2, sl 1, K1, psso, K to last 4 sts, K2tog, K2.
103 [111: 119: 125: 131: 139] sts.
Working all decs as set by last 2 rows, dec 1 st at each end of next 3 [3: 3: 1: 1: 1] rows, then on foll 2 [2: 2: 3: 2: 2] alt rows.
93 [101: 109: 117: 125: 133] sts.
Cont straight until armholes meas 24 [25: 26: 27: 28: 29] cm, ending with RS facing for next row.
Shape shoulders and back neck
Cast off 8 [10: 11: 12: 13: 14] sts at beg of next 2 rows.
77 [81: 87: 93: 99: 105] sts.
Next row (RS): Cast off 9 [10: 11: 12: 13: 15] sts, P until there are 12 [13: 14: 16: 17: 18] sts on right hand needle, turn and leave rem sts on a stitch holder.
Work each side of neck separately.
Next row (WS): Cast off 3 sts, K to end.
Cast off rem 9 [10: 11: 13: 14: 15] sts.
With RS facing, rejoin yarn to rem sts, cast off centre 35 [35: 37: 37: 39: 39] sts, P to end.

Complete to match first side reversing shapings.

FRONT

Work as given for back to ★★.
Row 1 (RS): P53 [56: 59: 62: 65: 68], (K1, P1,) 4 times, K1, P to end.
Row 2: K53 [56: 59: 62: 65: 68], (P1, K1,) 4 times, P1, K to end.
Row 3: P53 [56: 59: 62: 65: 68], K1, P1, T5B, P1, K1, P to end.
Row 4: As row 2.
Rows 5 to 8: Rep rows 1 and 2 twice.
These 8 rows form patt.
Cont in patt as set until front matches back to shape armholes, ending with RS facing for next row.
Shape armholes
Cast off 4 [3: 2: 2: 2: 1] sts at beg of next 2 rows.
107 [115: 123: 129: 135: 143] sts.
Next row (RS): P2, P2tog, P to last 4 sts, P2togtbl, P2.
Next row: K2, sl 1, K1, psso, K to last 4 sts, K2tog, K2.
103 [111: 119: 125: 131: 139] sts.
Working all decs as set by last 2 rows, dec 1 st at each end of next 3 [3: 3: 1: 1: 1] rows, then on foll 2 [2: 2: 3: 2: 2] alt rows.
93 [101: 109: 117: 125: 133] sts.
Work 1 row, ending with RS facing for next row.
Divide for neck
Next row (RS): P40 [44: 48: 52: 56: 60], P2togtbl, (K1, P1) twice, turn and leave rem sts on stitch holder.
Work each side of neck separately.
Next row (WS): (K1, P1) twice, K to end.
45 [49: 53: 57: 61: 65] sts.
Last 2 rows set neck decs and 4 sts in rib at neck edge.
Dec 1 st at neck edge as before on next row, then on 15 [15: 16: 16: 17: 17] foll alt rows, then 3 foll 4th rows.
26 [30: 33: 37: 40: 44] sts.
Cont straight until left front matches back to shape shoulders, ending with RS facing for next row.

Shape shoulder

Cast off 8 [10: 11: 12: 13: 14] sts at beg of next row, then 9 [10: 11: 12: 13: 15] sts at beg of foll alt row.

Work 1 row.

Cast off rem 9 [10: 11: 13: 14: 15] sts.

With RS facing, slip centre st onto a stitch holder, rejoin yarn to rem sts, (P1, K1) twice, P2tog, P to end.

Complete to match first side reversing shapings.

SLEEVES

Using 5mm (US 8) needles cast on 47 [49: 51: 53: 55: 57] sts.

Work 14 rows in rib as given for back dec 1 st at centre of last of these rows. 46 [48: 50: 52: 54: 56] sts.

Change to 5½mm (US 9) needles.

Beg with a P row, cont in rev st st shaping sides by inc 1 st at each end of 3rd row then on every foll 4th [4th: 4th: 4th: 6th: 6th] row to 68 [66: 62: 60: 98: 94] sts, then every foll 6th [6th: 6th: 6th: –: 8th] row to 90 [92: 94: 96: –: 100] sts.

Cont straight until sleeve meas 52 [54: 56: 58: 60: 62] cm, ending with RS facing for next row.

Shape top

Cast off 4 [3: 2: 2: 2: 1] sts at beg of next 2 rows.

82 [86: 90: 92: 94: 98] sts.

Dec 1 st at each end of next 5 rows, then on foll 9 [9: 9: 10: 11: 11]

alt rows, then every row to 40 sts.

Cast off 10 sts at beg of next 2 rows.

Cast off rem 20 sts.

MAKING UP

Press as described on the information page.

Join right shoulder seam.

Neckband

With RS facing and using 5mm (US 8) needles, pick up and knit 44 [44: 46: 46: 48: 48] sts down left side of neck, K centre st from stitch holder and mark this st, pick up and knit 44 [44: 46: 46: 48: 48] sts up right side of neck and 40 [40: 42: 42: 44: 44] sts from back neck. 129 [129: 135: 135: 141: 141] sts.

Row 1 (WS): ★ K1, P1, rep from ★ to 2 sts before marked st, rib 2 tog, P marked st, rib2tog, ★ P1, K1, rep from ★ to end. 127 [127: 133: 133: 139: 139] sts.

This row sets rib and v neck shaping.

Work 7 rows more in rib, dec 1 st at either side of marked st as before, ending with **WS** facing for next row. 113 [113: 119: 119: 125: 125] sts.

Cast off in rib dec 1 st at each side of centre st as before.

See information page for finishing instructions, setting in sleeves using the shallow set-in method.

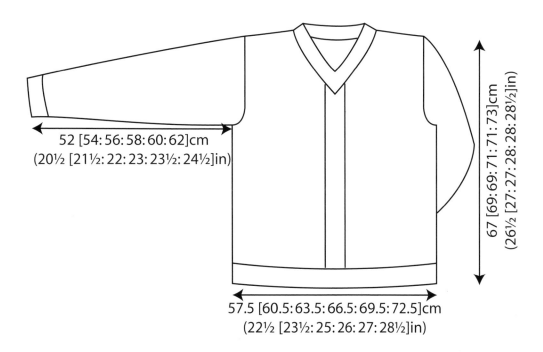

52 [54: 56: 58: 60: 62]cm
(20½ [21½: 22: 23: 23½: 24½]in)

67 [69: 69: 71: 71: 73]cm
(26½ [27: 27: 28: 28: 28½]in)

57.5 [60.5: 63.5: 66.5: 69.5: 72.5]cm
(22½ [23½: 25: 26: 27: 28½]in)

information

TENSION

Obtaining the correct tension is perhaps the single factor which can make the difference between a successful garment and a disastrous one. It controls both the shape and size of an article, so any variation, however slight, can distort the finished garment. Different designers feature in our books and it is their tension, given at the start of each pattern, which you must match. We recommend that you knit a square in pattern and/or stocking stitch (depending on the pattern instructions) of perhaps 5 - 10 more stitches and 5 - 10 more rows than those given in the tension note. Mark out the central 10cm square with pins. If you have too many stitches to 10cm try again using thicker needles, if you have too few stitches to 10cm try again using finer needles. Once you have achieved the correct tension your garment will be knitted to the measurements indicated in the size diagram shown at the end of the pattern.

SIZING & SIZE DIAGRAM NOTE

The instructions are given for the smallest size. Where they vary, work the figures in brackets for the larger sizes. One set of figures refers to all sizes. Included with most patterns in this magazine is a 'size diagram', of the finished garment and its dimensions. The measurment shown at the bottom of each 'size diagram' shows the garment width 2.5cm below the armhole shaping. To help you choose the size of garment to knit please refer to the sizing guide.

KNITTING WITH COLOUR

There are two main methods of working colour into a knitted fabric: Intarsia and Fairisle techniques. The first method produces a single thickness of fabric and is usually used where a colour is only required in a particular area of a row and does not form a repeating pattern across the row, as in the fairisle technique.

Intarsia: The simplest way to do this is to cut short lengths of yarn for each motif or block of colour used in a row. Then joining in the various colours at the appropriate point on the row, link one colour to the next by twisting them around each other where they meet on the wrong side to avoid gaps. All ends can then either be darned along the colour join lines, as each motif is completed or then can be " knitted-in" to the fabric of the knitting as each colour is worked into the pattern. This is done in much the same way as "weaving- in" yarns when working the Fairisle technique and does save time darning-in ends. It is essential that the tension is noted for Intarsia as this may vary from the stocking stitch if both are used in the same pattern.

Fair isle type knitting: When two or three colours are worked repeatedly across a row, strand the yarn not in use loosely behind the stitches being worked. If you are working with more than two colours, treat the "floating" yarns as if they were one yarn and always spread the stitches to their correct width to keep them elastic. It is advisable not to carry the stranded or "floating" yarns over more than three stitches at a time, but to weave them under and over the colour you are working. The "floating" yarns are therefore caught at the back of the work.

FINISHING INSTRUCTIONS

After working for hours knitting a garment, it seems a great pity that many garments are spoiled because such little care is taken in the pressing and finishing process. Follow the following tips for a truly professional-looking garment.

PRESSING

Block out each piece of knitting and following the instructions on the ball band press the garment pieces, omitting the ribs. Tip: Take special care to press the edges, as this will make sewing up both easier and neater. If the ball band indicates that the fabric is not to be pressed, then covering the blocked out fabric with a damp white cotton cloth and leaving it to stand will have the desired effect. Darn in all ends neatly along the selvage edge or a colour join, as appropriate.

STITCHING

When stitching the pieces together, remember to match areas of colour and texture very carefully where they meet. Use a seam stitch such as back stitch or mattress stitch for all main knitting seams and join all ribs and neckband with mattress stitch, unless otherwise stated.

CONSTRUCTION

Having completed the pattern instructions, join left shoulder and neckband seams as detailed above. Sew the top of the sleeve to the body of the garment using the method detailed in the pattern, referring to the appropriate guide:

Straight cast-off sleeves: Place centre of cast-off edge of sleeve to shoulder seam. Sew top of sleeve to body, using markers as guidelines where applicable.

Square set-in sleeves: Place centre of cast-off edge of sleeve to shoulder seam. Set sleeve head into armhole, the straight sides at top of sleeve to form a neat right-angle to cast-off sts at armhole on back and front.

Shallow set-in sleeves: Place centre of cast off edge of sleeve to shoulder seam. Match decreases at beg of armhole shaping to decreases at top of sleeve. Sew sleeve head into armhole, easing in shapings.

Set- in sleeves: Place centre of cast-off edge of sleeve to shoulder seam. Set in sleeve, easing sleeve head into armhole.

Join side and sleeve seams.
Slip stitch pocket edgings and linings into place.
Sew on buttons to correspond with buttonholes.
Ribbed welts and neckbands and any areas of garter stitch should not be pressed.

CHART NOTE

Many of the patterns in the book are worked from charts. Each square on a chart represents a stitch and each line of squares a row of knitting. Each colour used is given a different letter and these are shown in the materials section, or in the key alongside the chart of each pattern. When working from the charts, read odd rows (K) from right to left and even rows (P) from left to right, unless otherwise stated. When working lace from a chart it is important to note that all but the largest size may have to alter the first and last few stitches in order not to lose or gain stitches over the row.

WORKING A LACE PATTERN

When working a lace pattern it is important to remember that if you are unable to work both the increase and corresponding decrease and vica versa, the stitches should be worked in stocking stitch.

abbreviations & experience ratings

K	knit	RS	right side
P	purl	WS	wrong side
st(s)	stitch(es)	sl 1	slip one stitch
inc	increas(e)(ing)	psso	pass slipped stitch over
dec	decreas(e)(ing)	p2sso	pass 2 slipped stitches over
st st	stocking stitch (1 row K, 1 row P)	tbl	through back of loop
g st	garter stitch (K every row)	M1	make one stitch by picking up horizontal loop before next stitch and knitting into back of it
beg	begin(ning)		
foll	following	M1P	make one stitch by picking up horizontal loop before next stitch and purling into back of it
rem	remain(ing)		
rev st st	reverse stocking stitch (1 row K , 1 row P)	yfwd	yarn forward
rep	repeat	yrn	yarn round needle
alt	alternate	meas	measures
cont	continue	0	no stitches, times or rows
patt	pattern	–	no stitches, times or rows for that size
tog	together	yo	yarn over needle
mm	millimetres	yfrn	yarn forward round needle
cm	centimetres	wyib	with yarn at back
in(s)	inch(es)	sl2togK	slip 2 stitches together knitways

Easy, straight forward knitting

Suitable for the average knitter

For the more experienced knitter

sizing guide

Our sizing now conforms to standard clothing sizes. Therefore if you buy a standard size 12 in clothing, then our size 12 or medium patterns will fit you perfectly.

Dimensions in the charts shown are body measurements, not garment dimensions, therefore please refer to the measuring guide to help you to determine which is the best size for you to knit.

CASUAL SIZING GUIDE FOR WOMEN

As there are some designs that are intended to fit more generously, we have introduced our casual sizing guide. The designs that fall into this group can be recognised by the size range: Small, Medium, Large & Xlarge. Each of these sizes cover two sizes from the standard sizing guide, ie. Size S will fit sizes 8/10, size M will fit sizes 12/14 and so on. The sizing within this chart is also based on the larger size within the range, ie. M will be based on size 14.

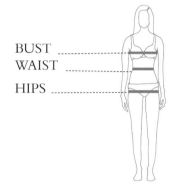

BUST
WAIST
HIPS

UK SIZE DUAL SIZE	S 8/10	M 12/14	L 16/18	XL 20/22	XXL 24/26	
To fit bust	32 – 34	36 – 38	40 – 42	44 – 46	48-50	inches
	81 – 86	91 – 97	102 – 107	112 – 117	122/127	cm
To fit waist	24 – 26	28 – 30	32 – 34	36 – 38	40-42	inches
	61 – 66	71 – 76	81 – 86	91 – 97	102-107	cm
To fit hips	34 – 36	38 – 40	42 – 44	46 – 48	50-52	inches
	86 – 91	97 – 102	107 – 112	117 – 122	127-132	cm

STANDARD SIZING GUIDE FOR MEN

UK SIZE EUR Size	S 50	M 52	L 54	XL 56	XXL 58	2XL 60	
To fit chest	40	42	44	46	48	50	inches
	102	107	112	117	122	127	cm
To fit waist	32	34	36	38	40	42	inches
	81	86	91	97	102	107	cm

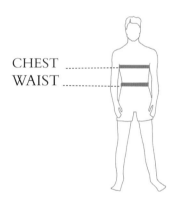

CHEST
WAIST

MEASURING GUIDE

For maximum comfort and to ensure the correct fit when choosing a size to knit, please follow the tips below when checking your size. Measure yourself close to your body, over your underwear and don't pull the tape measure too tight!

Bust/chest – measure around the fullest part of the bust/chest and across the shoulder blades.

Waist – measure around the natural waistline, just above the hip bone.

Hips – measure around the fullest part of the bottom.

If you don't wish to measure yourself, note the size of a favourite jumper that you like the fit of. Our sizes are now comparable to the clothing sizes from the major high street retailers, so if your favourite jumper is a size Medium or size 12, then our casual size Medium and standard size 12 should be approximately the same fit.

To be extra sure, measure your favourite jumper and then compare these measurements with the Rowan size diagram given at the end of the individual instructions.

Finally, once you have decided which size is best for you, please ensure that you achieve the tension required for the design you wish to knit.

Remember if your tension is too loose, your garment will be bigger than the pattern size and you may use more yarn. If your tension is too tight, your garment could be smaller than the pattern size and you will have yarn left over.

Furthermore if your tension is incorrect, the handle of your fabric will be too stiff or floppy and will not fit properly. It really does make sense to check your tension before starting every project.

AUSTRALIA: Australian Country Spinners, Pty Ltd, Level 7, 409 St. Kilda Road, Melbourne Vic 3004. Tel: 03 9380 3830 Fax: 03 9820 0989 Email: sales@auspinners.com.au

AUSTRIA: Coats Harlander GmbH, Autokaderstrasse 31, A -1210 Wien. Tel: (01) 27716 – 0   Fax: (01) 27716 - 228

BELGIUM: Coats Benelux, Ring Oost 14A, Ninove, 9400, Belgium Tel: 0346 35 37 00 Email: sales.coatsninove@coats.com

CANADA: Westminster Fibers Inc, 165 Ledge St, Nashua, NH03060 Tel: (1 603) 886 5041 / 5043   Fax: (1 603) 886 1056 Email: rowan@westminsterfibers.com

CHINA: Coats Shanghai Ltd, No 9 Building , Baosheng Road, Songjiang Industrial Zone, Shanghai. Tel: (86- 21) 5774 3733   Fax: (86-21) 5774 3768

DENMARK: Coats Danmark A/S, Nannasgade 28, 2200 Kobenhavn N Tel: (45) 35 86 90 50   Fax: (45) 35 82 15 10 Email: info@hpgruppen.dk Web: www.hpgruppen.dk

FINLAND: Coats Opti Oy, Ketjutie 3, 04220 Kerava Tel: (358) 9 274 871   Fax: (358) 9 2748 7330 Email: coatsopti.sales@coats.com

FRANCE: Coats France / Steiner Frères, SAS 100, avenue du Général de Gaulle, 18 500 Mehun-Sur-Yèvre Tel: (33) 02 48 23 12 30   Fax: (33) 02 48 23 12 40

GERMANY: Coats GMbH, Kaiserstrasse 1, D-79341 Kenzingen Tel: (49) 7644 8020   Fax: (49) 7644 802399 Web: www.coatsgmbh.de

HOLLAND: Coats Benelux, Ring Oost 14A, Ninove, 9400, Belgium Tel: 0346 35 37 00 Email: sales.coatsninove@coats.com

HONG KONG: Coats China Holdings Ltd, 19/F Millennium City 2, 378 Kwun Tong Road, Kwun Tong, Kowloon Tel: (852) 2798 6886   Fax: (852) 2305 0311

ICELAND: Storkurinn, Laugavegi 59, 101 Reykjavik Tel: (354) 551 8258 Email: storkurinn@simnet.is

ITALY: Coats Cucirini s.r.l., Via Sarca 223, 20126 Milano Tel: 800 992377   Fax: 0266111701 Email: servizio.clienti@coats.com

KOREA: Coats Korea Co Ltd, 5F Kuckdong B/D, 935-40 Bangbae- Dong, Seocho-Gu, Seoul Tel: (82) 2 521 6262.   Fax: (82) 2 521 5181

LEBANON: y.knot, Saifi Village, Mkhalissiya Street 162, Beirut Tel: (961) 1 992211 Fax: (961) 1 315553 Email: y.knot@cyberia.net.lb

LUXEMBOURG: Coats Benelux, Ring Oost 14A, Ninove, 9400, Belgium Tel: 054 318989 Email: sales.coatsninove@coats.com

MEXICO: Estambres Crochet SA de CV, Aaron Saenz 1891-7, Monterrey, NL 64650 Mexico Tel: +52 (81) 8335-3870

NEW ZEALAND: ACS New Zealand, 1 March Place, Belfast, Christchurch Tel: 64-3-323-6665 Fax: 64-3-323-6660

NORWAY: Coats Knappehuset AS, Pb 100 Ulset, 5873 Bergen Tel: (47) 55 53 93 00   Fax: (47) 55 53 93 93

SINGAPORE: Golden Dragon Store, 101 Upper Cross Street #02-51, People's Park Centre, Singapore 058357 Tel: (65) 6 5358454   Fax: (65) 6 2216278   Email: gdscraft@hotmail.com

SOUTH AFRICA: Arthur Bales PTY, PO Box 44644, Linden 2104 Tel: (27) 11 888 2401   Fax: (27) 11 782 6137

SPAIN: Oyambre, Pau Claris 145, 80009 Barcelona. Tel: (34) 670 011957   Fax: (34) 93 4872672 Email: oyambre@oyambreonline.com

Coats Fabra, Santa Adria 20, 08030 Barcelona Tel: 932908400   Fax: 932908409 Email: atencion.clientes@coats.com

SWEDEN: Coats Expotex AB, Division Craft, Box 297, 401 24 Goteborg Tel: (46) 33 720 79 00   Fax: 46 31 47 16 50

SWITZERLAND: Coats Stroppel AG, Stroppelstr.16 CH -5300 Turgi (AG) Tel: (41) 562981220   Fax: (41) 56 298 12 50

TAIWAN: Cactus Quality Co Ltd, P.O.Box 30 485, Taipei, Taiwan, R.O.C., Office: 7FL-2, No 140, Roosevelt Road, Sec 2, Taipei, Taiwan, R.O.C. Tel: 886-2-23656527 Fax: 886-2-23656503   Email: cqcl@m17.hinet.net

THAILAND: Global Wide Trading, 10 Lad Prao Soi 88, Bangkok 10310 Tel: 00 662 933 9019 Fax: 00 662 933 9110 Email: theneedleworld@yahoo.com

U.S.A.: Westminster Fibers Inc, 165 Ledge St, Nashua, NH03060 Tel: (1 603) 886 5041 / 5043   Fax: (1 603) 886 1056 Email: rowan@westminsterfibers.com

U.K: Rowan, Green Lane Mill, Holmfirth, West Yorkshire, England HD9 2DX Tel: +44 (0) 1484 681881   Fax: +44 (0) 1484 687920 Email: mail@knitrowan.com Web: www.knitrowan.com

For stockists in all other countries please contact Rowan for details

Photographer · Chloe Mallett (One Photographic)
Art Direction & Sylist · Rowan
Hair & Make-up · Frances Prescott (One Photographic)
Models · Sophie Cook & Josh McGhee (Models 1) & Abigail Gott (Select Model Management)

Design Layout · Rowan

Handknitters · Violet Ellis, Wendy Shipman, Heather Esswood, Elsie Eland, Arna Ronan, Joyce Sledmore, Glennis Garnet, Pat Garden, Mary Potter, Marjorie Pickering, Honey Ingram, Yvonne Rawlinson, Wendy Stevens.

Many Thanks · Melin Tregwynt for the loan of the backdrop fabrics; please see www.melintregwynt.co.uk for further details or tel: +44(0)1348 891 255

Buttons · Bedecked Ltd, 1 Castle Wall, Back Fold, Hay-On-Wye, Via Hereford, HR3 5EQ
shop tel: 01497 822769
web: www.bedecked.co.uk
email: thegirls@bedecked.co.uk

Bedecked
fine trimmings

First published in Great Britain in 2009 by Rowan Yarns Ltd, Green Lane Mill, Holmfirth, West Yorkshire, England, HD9 2DX
Internet: www.knitrowan.com
© Copyright Rowan 2009
British Library Cataloguing in Publication Data Rowan Yarns - Lima Collection
ISBN 978-1-906007-70-6